D1121843

Autobiography
as
Activism

Three **Black Women** of the Sixties

Margo V. Perkins

University Press of Mississippi
Jackson

www.upress.state.ms.us

Copyright © 2000 by University Press of Mississippi
All rights reserved
Manufactured in the United States of America

08 07 06 05 04 03 02 01 00   4 3 2 1

Library of Congress Cataloging-in-Publication Data

Perkins, Margo V.
Autobiography as activism : three Black women of the Sixties /
Margo V. Perkins.
    p.   cm.
Based on the author's thesis (Cornell University).
Includes bibliographical references and index.
ISBN 1-57806-230-6 (alk. paper)   ISBN 1-57806-264-0 (pbk.: alk. paper)
    1. American prose literature—Afro-American authors—History and
criticism.   2. Afro-American women political activists—Biography—
History and criticism.   3. American prose literature—Women authors—
History and criticism.   4. Afro-Americans—Biography—History and
criticism.   5. Davis, Angela Yvonne, 1944– Angela Davis.   6. Brown,
Elaine, 1943– Taste of power.   7. Shakur, Assata. Assata.
8. Autobiography—Afro-American authors.   9. Autobiography—
Women authors.   I. Title.
PS366.A35 P37 2000
305.48'896073'00922 21—dc21   99-040057

British Library Cataloging-in-Publication Data available

This work is dedicated to my parents,
Reba and Robert Perkins,
and to my aunt, Helen Wilson,
with love and appreciation

Contents

Acknowledgments

In completing *Autobiography as Activism: Three Black Women of the Sixties*, I relied on the support—material and emotional—of many good people. The journey from dissertation to book has been even more challenging than I had imagined. I want to thank my family (immediate and extended) for insisting that it could and should be done; their enthusiasm was there even when my own seemed to ebb. Special thanks to my gracious editor at the University Press of Mississippi, Seetha Srinivasan, who has demonstrated the patience of Job. Her interest, thoughtful advice, and gentle but persistent nudging throughout the revising and revisioning process convinced me that there really was a book in there somewhere. The generous critical feedback I received from Kari J. Winter at the University of Vermont helped me to begin crafting that book. Her comments on the dissertation, and later, on the revised manuscript, were invaluable. I am fortunate, as well, for the meticulous eye of Evan Young, whose useful suggestions and impeccable copyediting did much to improve the manuscript's flow.

For all of their helpful comments on drafts along the way, I am deeply indebted to the spirited members of my writing group at Trinity College: Joan Hedrick, Jane Nadel-Klein, and Barbara Sicherman. They managed to call my attention back to the forest when it seemed that all I could see were the trees. I am thankful for the support of many other Trinity colleagues as well, especially Jim Miller (whose presence on campus I miss), Jan Cohn for very helpful feedback on early outlines of the book, Ron Thomas, Jerry Watts, Fred Pfeil, Dina Anselmi, Cheryl Greenberg, and Lori Waite. I also appreciate Johnny Williams for reminding me to stay on task amidst the never-ending barrage of potential distractions, and W. S. Tkweme for providing wonderful distractions amidst the never-ending barrage of tasks. Finally, the enthusiasm of my students in AMST 334: *Autobiographies of the Black Power Movement* (fall 1995) continually renewed my own interest in the material.

For their work advising the dissertation that became the book, I owe special thanks to my graduate committee at Cornell University: Molly Hite (my dedicated chair), Kathryn Shanley, Harryette Mullen, and Lois Brown. At Cornell, James Turner was also a tremendous resource, as were Kenneth McClane and Micere Mugo. For their work in the trenches, I will be forever grateful to my truly amazing dissertation writing group: Rosetta Haynes, Elizabeth Davey, and Shuchi Kapila. Thanks also to my other buddies—Esther Hughes, Rayfield Waller, Yolanda Flores, Ayele Bekerie, and Eric Acree—for intellectual support and fellowship along the way.

Before Cornell, there was Spelman. I wish to express gratitude to my former professors there whose individual and collective examples have been the inspiration for my interest in the legacies of the three remarkable warrior women I've chosen to study herein. Although I am grateful to many, I would be remiss if I neglected to acknowledge individually my mentor, Gloria Wade-Gayles. In so many ways, her brilliance, creativity, and passion for both life and literature continue to awe and inspire me. I count her friendship among my many blessings in this life. I also will always be indebted to Judy Gebre-Hiwet, who first taught me what it means to be a critical reader *and* writer; Beverly Guy-Sheftall and Jacqueline Jones-Royster, who together brought me into SAGE; and to "Sister President," Johnetta Cole, whose generosity, dynamic leadership, and expressed faith in me have left a lasting impression.

Last but certainly not least, I am grateful to the Ford Foundation and to the Cornell Office of Minority Affairs under Dean Eleanor Reynolds. Their generous financial support enabled me to complete the dissertation that became the premise for this book. If there are still others whose assistance I have failed to acknowledge, please know that the oversight is unintentional. Whatever merits exist in this work must be credited in large part to the many who helped along the way. In turn, I accept full responsibility for whatever errors and shortcomings may remain.

Introduction

Thirty years after its demise, both the story and the legacy of the Black Power Movement in the United States remain deeply contested. The recent proliferation of works by or about the period from the late 1960s through the early 1970s coincides with the first historical moment in which the country has gained enough emotional and intellectual distance to prepare for thoughtful, if not yet dispassionate, assessments of this turbulent era. An outgrowth of the Civil Rights Movement, the Black Power Movement was the logical response to America's continued recalcitrance and oppression of African Americans despite a protracted and well-orchestrated campaign of nonviolent social protest. As an older generation gave way to a newly energized, idealistic, and decidedly impatient younger one, the call for civil rights that marked the mid-1950s through the early 1960s was rapidly eclipsed by the more militant call for Black Power. Although Martin Luther King Jr.'s popularity among young northern Blacks had already begun to wane by the mid-1960s, his assassination in April 1968 jolted and enraged even those who had become disillusioned with his determined adherence to nonviolent ideology. For many, King's death was a catalyst. If Dr. King could be so brutally murdered, many reasoned, there was little hope for a nonviolent solution to America's race problem. Black nationalist ideologies, which were already circulating in many Black communities, gained ascendancy, as activists of the late 1960s shifted their demand from civil to *human* rights.

Current popular interest in the Black Power Movement, which has come to focus largely on the Black Panther Party, seems to reflect the existence today of a growing desire to reclaim an oppositional or counterhegemonic voice that challenges the status quo. Frustration created by the resurfacing of overt racism and the systematic erosion, during the

1980s and 1990s, of affirmative action and other progressive policies that
have enabled substantive social, political, and economic gains by African
Americans, other ethnic minorities, and White women has furnished
the context for a renewed interest in oppositional rhetoric and practice.
My work on *Autobiography as Activism* comes out of this context. It is
both a product of and a complement to the current surge of popular
interest in the political and countercultural movements of the 1960s,
and the Black Power Movement in particular.

This book focuses on the kind of cultural work activists' narratives
do. Activists' texts give voice to oppositional or counterhegemonic ways
of knowing that repeatedly invite readers to challenge their own assumptions and level of comfort with the status quo. Reading the autobiographies of political activists introduces readers to what radical educator
Henry Giroux has referred to as a "language of empowerment." In
Schooling for Democracy: Critical Pedagogy in the Modern Age, he explains
that introducing individuals to a language of empowerment and radical
ethics "permits them to think about how community life should be constructed around a project of possibility" (Giroux, "Literacy," 166). Activists' narratives seize upon this project of possibility, advocating a
pedagogy of questioning and strategies of resistance that might easily be
applied to readers' own lives. I am interested in how Black Power activists use life-writing as an important tool for advancing political struggle.
This study consequently investigates: the different ways these activists
use autobiography to connect their own circumstances with those of
other activists across historical periods, their emphatic linking of the
personal and the political in agitating for transformative action, and
their constructing an alternative history that challenges hegemonic ways
of knowing.

In the last decade there have emerged a number of critical studies
about the Black Power era. These include William Van DeBurg's *New
Day in Babylon: The Black Power Movement and American Culture, 1965–
1975* (1992), Hugh Pearson's *The Shadow of the Panther: Huey Newton
and the Price of Black Power in America* (1994), and most recently Charles
Jones's edited volume, *The Black Panther Party Reconsidered* (1998). Of
the studies addressing the period that have been published to date, however, none has focused primarily on activists' autobiographies *as texts*.

Certainly, those writing histories of the Movement have drawn on the autobiographies as important resources in reconstructing the era, but analysis of the autobiographies themselves has not been the primary objective. *Autobiography as Activism* differs from these studies in that it is *not* a history of the Movement or of the Black Panther Party, or even a history of women's involvement therein. Autobiography is an avowedly subjective enterprise that yields a narrow vista over a sprawling landscape. It is not terribly concerned with the inevitable limitations of its own field of view. In focusing on the autobiographies, then, I am ultimately less interested in an authoritative history of the Black Power Movement than in the multiplicity of stories, told differently by different individuals, that make up that history. Activists use life-writing to recreate themselves as well as the era they recount. Many things are at stake for them in this process. These things include control of the historical record, control over their own public images, and control over how the resistance movement in which they are involved is defined and portrayed. In the case of those narratives that are directly tied to impending struggle, activists may even be writing to save their own lives. In this study, I look at the women's sense of themselves as both bearing witness and building legacies.

That the 1960s are still, for those who were intimately involved in the political events of that era, a living history makes it both an exciting and a difficult period to write about. Exciting because many of the key players *are* still alive; difficult because the reality of living subjects means that the stories, themselves, are alive as well. They are being contested even as this study goes to press. The list of original and reissued texts since the late 1980s includes Assata Shakur's *Assata* (1987), Earl Anthony's *Spitting in the Wind* (1990), Elaine Brown's *A Taste of Power* (1992), David Hilliard's *This Side of Glory* (1993), Evelyn Williams's *Inadmissible Evidence* (1993), George Jackson's *Soledad Brother* (reprinted 1994), Huey Newton's *Revolutionary Suicide* (reprinted 1995), and William Brent's *Long Time Gone* (1996). Kathleen Cleaver is also reportedly at work on her memoir, tentatively titled *Love and War*. New stories continue to emerge that would seem to challenge or "correct" older ones. One might argue that there is a struggle within the struggle being waged for control of the historical record. On one level, this struggle consists of activists challenging the history of African American resistance as it has been recorded (or elided) by the dominant culture. On another level, this struggle is also about activists challenging *each other's* individual recollections of the Movement and the people involved. As people's lives and reputations were alternately made and shattered by the turbulent events of the time, the effort to seize control over how this history will be remembered is no small matter.

I have chosen to focus here on the women's narratives because so little has been written about women's experiences in 1960s nationalist struggle. Of the popular and scholarly attention the Black Power Movement has received in recent years, the focus has been almost exclusively on the lives of the major male figures. While now classic conversion narratives like *The Autobiography of Malcolm X* and Eldridge Cleaver's *Soul on Ice* have been used to illustrate the process by which Black Americans become radical subjects in the struggle against racist and classist oppression, relatively little attention has been given to the gendered nature of Malcolm's and Cleaver's experiences, respectively. To what extent, for instance, might the quality of gender role expectations, interpersonal relationships, and parenthood be experienced differently for men and women in activist struggle? In what ways might the process of coming to radical political consciousness differ for women and men? How might the particular obstacles and consequences they each encounter along the way be different? In short, how do the women's stories fill in, complement, challenge, or converse with the stories told by their male counterparts to create a more complex and polyvocal appreciation of the period and the activists involved? Although these questions have important implications, women's experiences both in and leading up to involvement in activist struggle, where they have differed qualitatively from men's, have been largely unexplored in the critical literature, either historical or literary. An examination of the first person narratives written by women activists is a good place to begin redressing this elision. The works by Angela Davis, Assata Shakur, and Elaine Brown are, to date, the only book-length autobiographies published by women on the front lines of the Black Power Movement.

Because the narratives by women activists implicitly address the question of how women become radical subjects in this society, their stories begin to demystify the process by which some Black women, in the context of ongoing racist and sexist oppression, have been (and continue to be) able to move from the social and discursive status of objects to active subjects, capable of transforming their environment. The authors' efforts to situate their own experiences within a structural analysis of race, class, and gender oppression, as well as their offering their lives as examples, consequently provide rare models of what African American feminist critic bell hooks has termed "radical Black female subjectivity." Collectively, the women's stories also testify to the kinds of gender issues that tend to arise in nationalist struggle cross-culturally. They call attention to internal contradictions between the liberation movement's professed ideals (i.e., the theory or rhetoric) and its practices: the call for the liberation of all oppressed people, for example, contrasted with the simultaneous perpetuation of regressive patriarchal norms and expectations. The insight afforded by such a critique is not only historically valuable, but instructive today as well, in terms of how activists wage contemporary liberation struggles.

Autobiography as Activism analyzes the characteristics of Davis's, Shakur's, and Brown's narratives with attention to the levels on which their autobiographies function as extensions of their activist work. Chapter 1, "I am We: Black Women Activists Writing Autobiography," begins with information about these three women's respective backgrounds and the particular political and historical contexts out of which their individual autobiographies emerge. Although there are noteworthy differences between these women in terms of their activists sensibilities, the manner in which they come into political activism, and even the style of their narratives, a number of striking similarities also emerge. These commonalities provide a compelling rationale for treating all three women's narratives in a single study. Collectively, their texts afford important insight into the quality and range of Black women's activism during the period. In this chapter I also discuss political autobiography as a distinct genre with significant implications for how we subsequently read, critique, and assimilate such works.

Because the women's narratives arise out of a long tradition of African American resistance writing and struggle, it is possible to situate their texts within a corpus of autobiographical writing that extends as far back as the emancipation narratives. When placed in this context, the women's works reveal compelling thematic continuities with these earlier texts. Chapter 2, "Literary Antecedents in the Struggle for Freedom," explores what these continuities signify and also how Davis, Shakur, and Brown draw strategically on the emancipation narratives to add urgency and poignancy to their own political circumstances and agendas.

In their respective narratives, Davis, Shakur, and Brown identify and "theorize" pivotal moments in their early experiences. They also chart their own political evolution from a naive/less sophisticated state of awareness to a point of heightened self-consciousness, understanding, and/or agency that culminates in a commitment to revolutionary activism. Chapter 3, "On Becoming: Activists' Reflections on Their Formative Experiences," addresses the women's reading of their early experiences with an eye toward demystifying the processes by which African American women move into revolutionary consciousness. Here I begin to identify some of the pedagogical aspects of the women's texts. This manner in which they self-consciously use their autobiographies to teach is further explored in chapter 4, where I focus on the women's efforts to teach about the history of the Movement and about the dynamics and manifestations of race, class, and gender oppression in America. Titled "Autobiography as Political/Personal Intervention," chapter 4 additionally explores the more personal issues at stake for activists who write their lives. In what ways, for instance, does autobiography become a means for activists to seize control over their own images, often distorted or maligned in the popular press? Autobiography becomes an opportunity for activists to tell their own side of the story, and sometimes (as I argue in the case of Brown's A Taste of Power) to reinvent themselves against their own (and others') memories of the past.

Although political autobiographical texts by Black male activists, including Eldridge Cleaver's Soul on Ice, Huey Newton's Revolutionary Suicide, George Jackson's Soledad Brother, Bobby Seale's A Lonely Rage, and David Hilliard's This Side of Glory, occasionally raise the issue of gender oppression and its impact on the Movement, their narratives (and actions described therein) generally recapitulate the very practices they profess to critique. For this reason, it becomes apparent that the nature of women's experiences and concerns in political struggle cannot be adequately assessed from reading the men's narratives alone. Chapter 5, "Gender and Power Dynamics in 1960s Black Nationalist Struggle," examines the politics of gender in liberation struggle as raised in the women's narratives. Davis's, Shakur's, and Brown's critiques of sexism as they experienced it in the Movement are discussed in the context of 1970s feminist discourse, with some attention to the tension between White and Black women's experiences as articulated, for example, in Toni Cade Bambara's groundbreaking volume of essays, *The Black Woman* (1970). The chapter concludes with a focus on *A Taste of Power*'s complex contemporary critique of the relationship between gender and power in nationalist struggle, and some of the implications for reassessing the Movement. Brown's text enables unprecedented insight into the psychosexual dimensions of power as it transpired within the highest echelons of the Black Panther Party.

Just as reading the women's texts against the men's may prompt us to rethink our earlier ways of knowing, reading later texts against earlier narratives can also expand our understanding of the era. Chapter 6, "Reading Intertextually: Black Power Narratives Then and Now," demonstrates how dialogical moments between texts by different writers contribute to a rich, polyvocal people's history of the Movement. This chapter includes a close reading of the literal dialogue between Angela Davis and George Jackson captured in their respective autobiographies, and an analysis of the implied dialogue enacted by Elaine Brown's and David Hilliard's more recent narratives as they respond to the stories told by earlier writers. Davis and Jackson's dialogue is centered around the appropriate roles for men and women in political struggle and the way in which each contributes to the other's political education. The focus on Brown and Hilliard (both of whom published their narratives many years after the Movement) explores the way writing functions for each as an act of self-recovery and reconciliation with the past.

Indeed, one of the most exciting aspects of reading several narratives of the period against each other is the way the texts begin to "hold conversation" with one another. Reading the women's and men's narratives together facilitates a more complex appreciation not only of the period but also of the individual writers/activists involved. In her own collection of autobiographical reflections, *Storyteller*, Leslie Marmon Silko perhaps expresses this phenomenon best when she poetically writes:

> As with any generation
> the oral tradition depends upon each person

listening and remembering a portion
and it is together—
all of us remembering what we have heard together—
that creates the whole story
the long story of the people. (Silko, 6)

Each person adding to the story, in the spirit of orature, transforms the story, which then belongs to all who participate in its telling. Silko's words are relevant to Davis's, Shakur's, and Brown's work in that all three women's narratives endeavor to capture and contribute to the shaping of a people's collective consciousness.

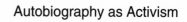

Autobiography as Activism

Credit: Associated Press

"I am We"
Black Women Activists
Writing Autobiography

As African American women intimately involved in the Black Power Movement in the United States during the late 1960s and early 1970s, Angela Davis, Assata Shakur, and Elaine Brown all shared a commitment to radical leftist politics and the building of a society free of race and class oppression. Disinclined to seek concessions within the existing socioeconomic structure, each participated in forms of revolutionary activism that sought to expose and aggressively challenge the structural underpinnings of race and class oppression in the United States. To date, they are the only women activists of the Black Power Movement to produce book-length autobiographies chronicling their experiences during this period. Because the nature of their activism as well as the character of their respective narratives is quite different, their stories taken collectively offer important insight into the range and quality of Black women's experiences in 1960s and 1970s revolutionary nationalist struggle.

Compared to Shakur and Brown, Angela Davis's exposure to leftist politics occurred early in life, first through her family and later as part of her formal education. The daughter of college-educated and politically active parents, Davis was granted a scholarship that enabled her to leave her birth town of Birmingham, Alabama, to attend Elizabeth Irwin, a private socialist high school in New York. There, she recalls her first encounter with the *Communist Manifesto*, as well as her participation in the activist Marxist-Leninist youth organization Advance. As a member of Advance, Davis took part in numerous peace and civil rights demonstrations. Following graduation from Elizabeth Irwin, Davis attended Brandeis University, where she received her undergraduate degree in French, and also became acquainted with the eminent philosopher Herbert Marcuse, who was later to have a profound influence on her political career. Davis's tenure at Brandeis included a year abroad at the Sorbonne in Paris, followed upon her graduation by a fellowship to study philosophy at Goethe University in Frankfurt. While in Germany, Davis participated in several rallies and demonstrations, most protesting U.S. involvement in the war in Vietnam. Lured back across the Atlantic by the dramatic events unfolding in the United States (associated with the shift in the Black liberation struggle from civil rights to Black Power), Davis determined to complete her doctorate in philosophy at the University of California, San Diego, where she could take active part in the struggle while continuing to pursue her studies.

Back in the States, Davis became involved with both the Student Nonviolent Coordinating Committee (SNCC) and John Floyd's Black Panther Political Party (BPPP). (Floyd's BPPP was not affiliated with Newton and Seale's Black Panther Party, originally known as the Black Panther Party for Self-Defense.) Although Davis's work on the west coast included interaction with Newton's Black Panther Party (BPP) as well, she decided in the end not to join that organization. Dissatisfied with the rampant sexism in the BPP and its tendency toward ad hoc political (re-)action, Davis states that she chose instead in 1968 to affiliate formally with the Che-Lumumba Club of the Communist Party USA. The Che-Lumumba Club was organized by and for Black members of the Party specifically to address the interests and needs of the Black liberation struggle. When Davis later became a professor at the University of California at Los Angeles (UCLA), her avowed membership in the Communist Party made her a target of the red-baiting campaign carried out by the Board of Regents under then-governor Ronald Reagan. In a case that drew widespread attention, Davis was eventually fired from her job. The chain of events that followed would catapult her onto the international scene. In August 1970, Davis became a wanted fugitive in the aftermath of Jon Jackson's failed Marin County Courtroom siege. Acquainted with Jackson and his family through her work on behalf of the Soledad Brothers Defense Committee, Davis was captured and formally charged by the FBI in October 1970 with murder, kidnapping, and conspiracy, as an accessory to Jackson's crime. For the next twenty-two months, Davis and her legal team, along with supporters in both the United States and abroad, worked diligently to secure her freedom.

Finally, on June 4, 1972, Davis was acquitted of all charges. Davis's narrative, titled *Angela Davis: An Autobiography*, published by Random House in 1974, was written largely while she was awaiting trial on charges associated with the Marin County incident. Appearing shortly after her acquittal, Davis's text as resistance literature is tied to her impending struggle. In the preface to her narrative, she asserts, for example, that she deliberately set out to write a "political autobiography" (xvi) that would (1) raise the consciousness of readers by helping them better understand the particular conditions that necessitated resistance struggle by African Americans and other oppressed groups, and (2) encourage others to join the struggle.

Assata Shakur's introduction to political activism was quite different from Davis's. Born JoAnne Byron and reared by her mother and stepfather, maternal grandparents, and maternal aunt, Shakur grew up in both Jamaica, New York, and Wilmington, North Carolina. Although a spirited nonconformist even as a child, Shakur indicates that it was not until her association with a group of African students on Columbia University's campus that she began to acquire political literacy. The students, who were highly conversant in international politics, schooled Shakur in U.S. foreign policy and the issues underlying the war in Vietnam. As her political consciousness expanded, Shakur increasingly sought ways to become involved in resistance struggle. As a student at the City College of New York, she enthusiastically immersed herself in campus and community activism. For a brief period she affiliated with the Harlem branch of the Black Panther Party, before becoming disillusioned with the group for its authoritarian leadership, as well as for many of the same issues Davis identified. Increasingly subjected to police harassment and surveillance for her activities, Shakur went underground to continue her activist work with the Black Liberation Army (BLA), an offshoot of the BPP. The BLA was organized by supporters of Eldridge Cleaver in the aftermath of the Newton-Cleaver split in the Party. While operating underground, Shakur first garnered national attention on May 2, 1973, when she and two other BLA activists, Zayd Shakur and Sundiata Acoli, were violently apprehended by state troopers as they traveled on the New Jersey Turnpike. One state trooper, Werner Foerster, and Zayd Shakur were killed in the incident; Shakur herself was seriously wounded. Over the next several months in police custody, Shakur was indicted on numerous charges, including armed robbery, murder, attempted murder, and kidnapping. In all instances except one, she was eventually acquitted or had the charges against her dismissed. On March 25, 1977, however, she was convicted of Foerster's death. Shakur served six years in prison, from the time of her apprehension in 1973 to her successful escape in 1979 from the Clinton Correctional Facility for Women in New Jersey. Granted political asylum in Cuba, Shakur continues to reside there today. Although she is technically free, her status in exile is precarious since she remains on the FBI's list of wanted fugitives. Consequently, while Shakur's autobiography, titled *Assata*, was published by Lawrence Hill & Co. in 1987 (eight years after her escape from prison and flight to Cuba), her text, like Davis's, remains bound to impending struggle. The publicity that accompanied her conference with Pope John Paul II during his historic visit to Cuba in January 1998, for instance, resulted in a renewed push by New Jersey Governor Christine Todd Whitman and other local politicians for Shakur's extradition.

Compared to Davis and Shakur, Elaine Brown came to political activism late in life. Although the daughter of a politically active mother (Dorothy Clark was involved in union organizing), Brown confesses that she had little interest in or insight into the racial struggles taking place around the country. This changed for Brown primarily as a result of her pivotal relationship with Jay Kennedy, a wealthy White writer she met after moving from her hometown of Philadelphia to Los Angeles in April 1965 at the age of twenty-two. She and Kennedy, thirty-three years her senior, were introduced at the Pink Pussycat, an upscale club where Brown was employed as a cocktail waitress. Brown credits Kennedy with profoundly influencing her political evolution. By 1967, Brown's commitment to rigorous self-education through reading and studying had led to her immersion in Los Angeles's Black activist scene. Although not herself a student, Brown joined the Black Student Alliance organized by sociology professor Harry Truly, at the Los Angeles campus of California State University. Brown became the Alliance's first representative to the Black Congress, an umbrella organization of groups with similar political agendas. Her work with the Congress exposed her to a wide circle of leftist activists both formally and loosely associated with the Congress. In April 1968, at the age of twenty-five, Brown formally joined the Southern California chapter of the Black Panther Party.

By 1969 she was serving as Deputy Minister of Information of the Los Angeles chapter. She was promoted to Minister of Information of the Party in 1971 (the first female appointment to the Central Committee), formally replacing Eldridge Cleaver (*Taste of Power*, 304). Unlike Shakur and Davis, whose respective associations with the Party were fleeting, Brown remained an active member until the organization's eventual demise in the late 1970s. Although many individuals (activists and scholars) date the Party's effective demise even before Brown assumed leadership of the organization, a small and shrinking cadre of the Party did continue well into the late 1970s. Pulled into the organization's innermost circle through her close association with its founder, Huey Newton, Brown became the first woman to lead the Party after Newton's flight to Cuba in 1974.

Aside from her work to bolster such Panther community initiatives as the Oakland Community Learning Center, Brown is also credited with changing the direction of the Party in its later years to include active participation in electoral politics. Brown herself ran twice, though unsuccessfully, for the Oakland City Council. The Party's backing of mayoral candidate Lionel Wilson and diligent work to register voters helped ensure Wilson's 1977 victory as the first African American mayor of Oakland. Wielding the Party's influence, Brown additionally was instrumental in ensuring that the proposed construction of the controversial Grove-Shafter highway extension included provisions for jobs to benefit the predominately Black surrounding community. Finally, by her own account, Brown also used her power as head of the Party to move other women into more influential and visible roles within the historically male-dominated organization. Brown's autobiography, *A Taste of Power: A Black Woman's Story*, published by Pantheon in 1992, was written in the years following her 1977 departure from the Party. The time separating the autobiography from the period of her most intense activism means that Brown's text is less connected to impending struggle than either Davis's or Shakur's. While Brown's narrative treats some of the same political issues as Davis's and Shakur's narratives do, she appears to enter into the autobiographical project with a substantially different sense of purpose. Writing in a different era as well as from the vantage point of greater retrospective distance, her focus on gender and power dynamics during the era constitutes a different kind of political witnessing than that found in the other women's narratives.

While the three writers' shared commitment to revolutionary ideals and struggle creates numerous commonalities between their texts, some attention is due the important differences between the women and their works. This includes attention to the different contexts in which their respective narratives emerge, the way each writer approaches/negotiates the politics of the autobiographical form, and the different motives that impel each woman to tell her story. One noteworthy difference is the degree of immediacy characterizing each of the works. The heteroglossia of Davis's and Shakur's narratives, for instance, highlight the way in which both narratives are connected to impending struggle. While Brown's autobiography is dedicated to her daughter, and to those who assisted in the manuscript's preparation, for example, the dedication that appears at the beginning of Davis's autobiography and the poem that opens Shakur's text both affirm resistance struggle in a way that self-consciously connects their narratives to each other as well as to those of other activists across historical periods. Davis dedicates her autobiography to her family, her comrades, and those who will continue fighting "until racism and class injustice are forever banished from our history." Shakur has no formal dedication, but begins her narrative with a six-stanza poem titled "Affirmation." The first part of the poem presents stark images of death and repression, which Shakur subsequently contrasts with her own spirited determination to embrace life in the face of death. Noting that barriers to freedom are meant to be broken down, Shakur declares:

> I believe in living.
> I believe in birth.
> I believe in the sweat of love
> and in the fire of truth.
> And I believe that a lost ship,
> steered by tired, seasick sailors,
> can still be guided home
> to port.

Loosely modeled in form after the Catholic "Apostle's Creed," the poem's content reveals Shakur's reverence for life, her faith in humanity, and her belief in the redemptive value of resistance struggle.

Shakur's and Davis's autobiographies are generally consistent with values and conventions embraced by numerous other activist autobiographers in the United States and abroad. The expectations that have come to govern activists writing their life stories are manifold. These expectations, which collectively shape a genre of writing I will call *political autobiography* (after Davis's coining of the term), are implicitly revealed in the work of other activists as well as critics of resistance literature. They include the following: (1) that the autobiographer will emphasize the story of the struggle over her own personal ordeals; (2) that she will use her own story both to document a history of the struggle and to further its political agenda; (3) that she will provide a voice for the voiceless; (4) that she will honor strategic silences in order to protect the integrity of the struggle as well as the welfare of other activists; (5) that she will expose oppressive conditions and the repressive tactics of the state; and (6) that she will use the autobiography as a form of political intervention, to educate as broad an audience as possible to the situation and issues at stake.

Consistent with these expectations, many activists who write their autobiographies tend to evince a relational understanding of self. This is marked by both a redefining of the self through the story of the Movement, and a notable uneasiness with the project of autobiography because of the genre's historical emphasis, within the Western literary tradition, on heroic individualism. Repeatedly, human rights activists cross-culturally insist that their individual plight not be read in isolation from the communities they represent. The narratives of Winnie Mandela of South Africa, Rigoberta Menchú of Guatemala, and Domitila Barrios of Bolivia are exemplary. Referring to her struggle against South African apartheid, Winnie Mandela remarks, in *Part of My Soul Went With Him*: "I have ceased a long time ago to exist as an individual. The ideals, the political goals I stand for, those are the ideals and goals of the people in this country" (Mandela, 26). Rigoberta Menchú's narrative similarly opens with emphasis on the extent to which her own experiences are paradigmatic of others'. She insists: "I'd like to stress that it's not only my life, it's also the testimony of my people. . . . The important thing is that what has happened to me has happened to many other people too: My story is the story of all poor Guatemalans" (Menchú, 1). Perhaps Domitila Barrios captures the ethos of their shared project best when she speaks of her own autobiography as the "personal experience of my people" (Barrios, 15).

Within the United States, political prisoner George Jackson, in "Recent Letters and An Autobiography" (a twenty-page narrative preceding the collection of letters that make up *Soledad Brother*), also noted that he found difficulty in complying with the request to furnish a brief autobiography. He explains: "I don't recognize uniqueness, not as it's applied to individualism, because it is too tightly tied into decadent capitalist culture" (Jackson, *Soledad*, 10). He goes on to acknowledge, however, that he knows no other way to account for his difference from other Black people around him. Rhetorically, he ponders: "But then how can I explain the runaway slave in terms that do not imply uniqueness?" In contrast to Angela Davis's vigorous attempts in the preface to her autobiography to downplay her uniqueness, Jackson seems more willing to openly acknowledge that he is both typical (in the sense that he shares the plight of other Black people under racist oppression) and atypical (in the sense that his resistance to oppression is both active and subversive). The uneasiness political autobiographers tend to experience with the personal "I" may even be symbolized in the lowercase "i" Assata Shakur uses throughout her narrative. Because the personal pronouns "she" and "he" are conventionally rendered in lowercase, Shakur's use of a small "i" suggests an understanding of self as neither more nor less important than any other.

Davis approaches the autobiographical project with a humility that comes close to apology. Her disclaimers are elaborate, the first appearing with the original publication in 1974 and the second appended, as she says, "nearly fifteen years" later (Davis, *Autobiography*, vii). In the original preface, Davis writes: "I felt that to write about my life, what I did, what I thought and what happened to me would require a posture of difference, an assumption that I was unlike other women—other Black women—and therefore needed to explain myself" (xv). Davis is most concerned that she not be viewed in isolation from the mass struggle with which she identifies, since she perceives that it is, in fact, the struggle that gives her speech legitimacy. In the introduction that appears with the book's second printing, Davis is less timid, though still inclined to qualify her decision to write. She explains: "I did not measure the events of my own life according to their possible personal importance. Rather I attempted to utilize the autobiographical genre to evaluate my life in accordance with what I considered to be the political significance of my experiences" (viii). With the advantage in the second preface of increased distance she is, however, confident that the work constitutes "an important piece of historical description and analysis of the late 1960s and early 1970s" (vii). Davis also uses the introduction to the second printing to mention her continued activist work up to the present (i.e., 1988), thus reestablishing her continued authority to write.

Like the uneasiness with or subjugation of the personal "I," other conventions and practices common to activists' texts tend to disrupt the kinds of values traditionally encoded in Western autobiographical practice. Of course, in recent years, the expectations for autobiography have undergone considerable changes owing in part to the contributions of feminist and poststructuralist theory and to scholarly attention to texts produced by writers outside the dominant culture. This notwithstanding, the conventional understanding of autobiography has been that it is the narrative ordering of an individual's life that illuminates, in the process, his or her uniqueness. It is, after all, this uniqueness that ostensibly entitles the prospective autobiographer to write in the first place. Autobiography by writers situated within (or influenced by) Western imperialist culture historically has taken as its impetus and focus the way in which the individual's life is distinguished from the lives of those around him. The assumption, then, is that the ideal autobiographical subject is that individual whose life achievements merit special recognition. The tendency of contemporary critics to cite—often for the purpose of problematizing—Georges Gusdorf's claims suggests that it was his writing in the 1950s about autobiography as a genre that truly exposed the ethos implicit in the Western autobiographical project. In his seminal essay, "Conditions and Limits of Autobiography," Gusdorf argued that "autobiography is not to be found outside of our cultural area: one would say that it expresses a concern peculiar to Western man, a concern that has been of good use in his systematic conquest of the universe" (Gusdorf, 29). He proposed that it is primarily the concern for preservation of self (the individual as he stands in relief to his environment) that motivates autobiography (29). In establishing a context (a series of prerequisites he termed "metaphysical preconditions"[1]) for the emergence of autobiography as a peculiarly Western (read White, middle-class, heterosexual, male) form, Gusdorf failed to consider the possibility that members of non-hegemonic communities might undertake the telling of their own life stories for different purposes. He further assumed that there is only one understanding of "self" (i.e., the individual as apart from his/her community) from which autobiography might be generated. Gusdorf's assumptions implicitly link autobiography to an imperialist project and also leave no space for cultural difference or ways of knowing outside of those he privileges. If Gusdorf's claims can be read as capturing the ethos of the Western autobiographical tradition, then Davis, Brown, and Shakur, like other writers of political autobiography, write—to varying degrees—against this tradition. For them, autobiography is a vehicle used less to explore and glorify their individual uniqueness than to examine those experiences that connect them to their communities.

Shakur is especially emphatic in affirming the importance of connection to community. In addition to using her autobiography to educate, to expose, to correct, and to document, she also takes the opportunity to acknowledge a community of support. Speaking in the aftermath of her ordeal, she explains: "There were many, many people who i never got to meet, even though they worked so hard on my behalf. And even though i never got a chance to thank all the Black people, white people, Third World people, all the students, feminists, revolutionaries, activists, etc., who worked on the case, i thank you now" (*Assata*, 246). Shakur's

---

[1] Gusdorf writes: "Autobiography becomes possible only under certain metaphysical preconditions. To begin with, at the cost of a cultural revolution humanity must have emerged from the mythic framework of traditional teachings and must have entered into the perilous domain of history. The man who takes the trouble to tell of himself knows that the present differs from the past and that it will not be repeated in the future; he has become more aware of differences than of similarities; given the constant change, given the uncertainty of events and of men, he believes it a useful and valuable thing to fix his own image so that he can be certain it will not disappear like all things in this world. History then would be the memory of a humanity heading toward unforeseeable goals, struggling against the breakdown of forms and of beings. Each man matters to the world, each life and each death; the witnessing of each about himself enriches the common cultural heritage" (30).

text repeatedly alludes to her sense of solidarity with others. She asserts, for instance, that "there was never a time, no matter what horrible thing i was undergoing, when i felt completely alone" (223). Shakur also affirms connection to community through her use of the roll call, a convention of the oral tradition that recalls the names of other freedom fighters who have gone before and celebrates their place in a continuum of struggle. Roll calls of persecuted and/or slain activists have the effect not only of deflecting attention away from the uniqueness of the individual, but also of giving voice to the stories of those who have been silenced (through detention, death, or denied access to public media). There are at least three such roll calls in *Assata*. In "To My People, July 4, 1973," an audiotape she recorded to be smuggled out of the prison by her lawyer, Shakur charges: "They call us [the Black Liberation Army and its supporters] murderers, but we did not murder Martin Luther King Jr., Emmett Till, Medgar Evers, Malcolm X, George Jackson, Nat Turner, James Chaney. . . . We did not murder, by shooting in the back, sixteen-year-old Clifford Glover" (50). "To My People" concludes with a dedication "in the spirit of Ronald Carter, William Christmas, Mark Clark, Mark Essex, Frank 'Heavy' Fields, Woodie Changa Olugbala Green, Fred Hampton, Lil' Bobby Hutton, George Jackson, Jonathan Jackson, James McClain, Harold Russell, Zayd Malik Shakur, [and] Anthony Kumu Olugbala White" (52). Shakur offers no detail to go with the names. Barbara Harlow aptly notes as one of the characteristics of resistance literature the demand such narratives "make on the reader in their historical referencing and the burden of historical knowledge such referencing enjoins" (Harlow, *Resistance*, 80). Shakur's roll call is foremost a gesture of giving names to the nameless (i.e., of insisting upon their humanity) and of resisting America's propensity for historical erasure or forced forgetting. Her memory of them is a reminder not to betray their sacrifice as well as a source of inspiration for her own activities. Shakur's catalog signifies both resistance and the state's continued violence against those engaged in human rights struggle. The names are entered into the record like court evidence, to be used against the power structure when the time arrives. Writing autobiography, for Shakur, is a way of collecting and consolidating this information, which would otherwise be widely dispersed (in newspaper accounts, court documents, political literature and propaganda, and personal correspondence) and effectively lost. Even in listing names without the corresponding histories or circumstances, Shakur preserves vital information. Her roll call, like a library catalog, gives readers and researchers a place to start. The names of known and little-known (i.e., outside certain circles) activists are similarly sprinkled throughout the pages of Davis's and Brown's narratives.

Brown's A *Taste of Power* provides a perfect complement to the works by Shakur and Davis because its ethos and scope are notably different. This is in part the result of a nearly twenty-year hiatus between Brown's last association with the Black Panther Party and the manuscript's publication. Certainly, the publication of A *Taste* eighteen years after Davis's text means that the work emerges onto a very different sociopolitical landscape. Perhaps the most substantial differences between Brown's narrative and the narratives by Davis and Shakur, though, are attributable to Brown's own activist sensibility. While Brown's narrative treats some of the same political issues as Davis's and Shakur's, she appears to enter into the autobiographical project with a very different sense of purpose. In many ways, Brown seems less concerned with writing a "political autobiography" (as Davis defines her project) than with reconciling the meaning of her own past involvement in political struggle. This is reflected both in her narrative's avowedly personal slant (her foregrounding—as opposed to subjugation—of the individual "I") and her transgressing of the kinds of strategic silences observed in other activists' texts.

The subjugation or displacement of the individual "I" found in Shakur's and Davis's autobiographies is absent in Brown's more recent reflections on her life during the same period. Brown's negotiation of this convention appears to be complicated by the factors that motivate her decision to write. That is, she is concerned less with downplaying the self as unique than with recuperating a sense of self/identity *apart from* the Movement, and the Black Panther Party, even as her activities and experiences therein constitute the focus of her narrative. This quality, along with the fact that Brown's text is, as Barbara Harlow puts it, "less embed[ded] in the historical and material conditions of [its] production" (Harlow, *Resistance*, 98), tends to distinguish Brown's text from Shakur's and Davis's as a different kind of political writing. This difference notwithstanding, A *Taste* raises significant theoretical and pedagogical issues that make its discussion alongside the narratives by Davis and Shakur appropriate and important. Furthermore, because Brown's text frequently transgresses the expectations associated with autobiographical writing by political activists, A Taste is also valuable for the way it effectively illuminates a significant limitation of political narratives like Davis's and Shakur's: the lack of insight afforded into the interior or emotional life of the writer.

Within the genre of political autobiography, there is little room for activists' exposure of their interior lives, since focus on aspects of the struggle always takes precedence. Readers are given little detail about the more personal, intrapsychic dimensions of involvement in radical political struggle. In transgressing some of the conventions of political autobiography, A Taste is unique in offering such insight. Even as A Taste is about Brown's activities as a revolutionary, it is also about her ambivalence regarding those activities. In this way, she presents perhaps a less romanticized version of what it means to be engaged in radical political work. Unlike either Davis or Shakur, Brown relays retrospectively several moments of uncertainty in her continuing activism, citing the stress, fear, and anxiety of operating under intense police surveillance and repression, of existing outside social norms and expectations, and of enduring reactionary gender expectations within the Black Panther Party itself as factors prompting her to question her continued commitment. Clearly the latter issue constitutes at least one reason why both Davis and Shakur eventually distanced themselves from the Party to continue their activist work. For them, however, continued activism was never a question; the only uncertainty they acknowledge concerned the form their future activism would take. Shakur asserts, for example: "The more active i became the more i liked it. It was like medicine, making me well, making me whole" (Assata, 189). In sharp contrast to Shakur's testimony, Brown characterizes her own experiences as marked by stress and psychic fragmentation. During her early years with the Party, she even resorted to Thorazine (an antipsychotic prescribed by a psychiatric social worker) as a means of escaping both the pressures and anxieties associated with her activist work, and her concomitant feelings of nonexistence, alienation, and displacement. Her eventual addiction prompted her to take an extended absence from the Party. There are thus several moments in the text where Brown admits to uncertainty about the life she has chosen, a move that, in many ways, deromanticizes what it means to be a revolutionary.

Given the extent to which Movement activists suffered massive repression at the hands of the state, it is curious that the reality of death and loss is not explored more extensively in their texts. Perhaps the reason is that any admission of emotional pain and devastation of that magnitude grants one's enemies too much satisfaction, since the most fundamental goal of oppression is to break the human spirit. In a recent dialogue with fellow activist Kathleen Cleaver, Davis recalls in reflecting on the period: "One of the things that we didn't do then was mourn. Our strength was often defined by our ability not to allow the death of someone we loved to set us back" (Cleaver and Davis, 160). For activists to explore this pain in the context of their autobiographies, then, would invite a kind of voyeurism that all of the writers seem to eschew as far as their own individual suffering is concerned. Referring to the loss represented by George Jackson's death, Davis writes: "the deeply personal pain I felt would have strangled me had I not turned it into a proper and properly placed rage. I could not dwell on my own loss" (*Autobiography*, 319). She goes on to describe the way in which she determined to use Jackson's death to renew her own commitment to continued struggle. Supplying detail elided from Davis's narrative, Bettina Aptheker (Davis's friend and attorney) notes that Davis, in prison at the time, was unable to sleep in the days following news of Jackson's death. Aptheker adds that Davis's resolve was, nevertheless, unshaken. She elaborates: "Overwhelmed with grief, her face ashen in shock, her eyes wet with unending tears, comprehending the magnitude of the loss with infinitely greater intensity than any of us, she could still write" (Aptheker, 42). Davis was, at the time, composing a public statement describing what Jackson had meant to the Movement.

Davis's determination to use Jackson's death to motivate her continued struggle is a sentiment echoed by Shakur in her poem, "Story." Both "Story," which closes chapter 1 of *Assata*, and Shakur's poem for Rema Olugbala, in chapter 11, capture well the way the pain of personal loss is transformed in political autobiography into something collectively empowering. Shakur's placement of "Story" (which follows her narration of her apprehension on the New Jersey Turnpike) suggests that Zayd Shakur is her intended addressee; however, the dynamic captured in the verse might well be applied to countless others killed in struggle. Her poem is the story of Zayd but also the story of the Movement. Succinctly, she writes: "You died. / I cried. / And kept on getting up. / A little slower. / And a lot more deadly" (*Assata*, 17). Revealing a determined forward progression, the short end-stopped lines suggest emotional restraint or containment. That all the lines in the poem are end-stopped, furthermore, seems to symbolize discrete and processional stages in contending with loss. The impact of loss here is acknowledged in two ways. The first is the speaker's grief ("I cried") and the concomitant drain of psychic and physical energy that accompanies violent repression (i.e., she comes back, but "A little slower"). The third and fifth lines of the poem, however, acknowledge the impact of loss in a different way: they announce the speaker's renewed determination not only to continue fighting, but to raise the ante in the process. It makes sense that with each loss there is less to lose; and those with the least to lose are always potentially the most dangerous in any society. As Martin Oppenheimer notes in *The Urban Guerrilla*, increased repression directed toward those who already suffer the most extreme systemic oppression tends to augment group resistance. Indeed, the Panthers' desire to embrace the Black urban underclass (the lumpen proletariat) was based on precisely this awareness. This desire, however, was consigned mostly to theory. As cultural critic Amiri Baraka notes, the Party consisted predominantly of *working-class* Blacks. Despite the Party's "romanticization" of the Lumpen, he argues (citing information published in the Kerner Commission Report on Civil Disorders) that the rebellions that characterized the late 1960s "by and large were led by working class blacks, not the lumpen, as has been falsely projected" (Baraka, 28).

In her poem for Rema Olugbala (untitled), Shakur illustrates the sense in which the spirit of the Movement transcends individuals. Olugbala was scheduled to be tried along with Shakur and Ronald Myers for an alleged bank robbery committed in Queens, New York, on August 23, 1971 (160). (Shakur and Myers were later acquitted.) Although Olugbala died in a failed prison escape, his spirit of resistance is immortalized not only in Shakur's poem but most importantly, in all of the Olugbalas (i.e., angry "youngbloods") to come who undoubtedly will pick up where he has left off. Shakur writes:

They think they killed you.
But i saw you yesterday.
All them youngbloods
musta gave you a transfusion.
All that strong blood.
All that rich blood.
All that angry blood
flowing through your veins
toward tomorrow. (164)

For Shakur, incarcerated at the time she learned of Olugbala's death, writing the poem is a means of rechannelling as well as overcoming her own potentially debilitating feelings of rage and sorrow.

While Davis's and Shakur's texts show how activists use the experience of loss to renew their commitment to revolutionary struggle, Brown's narrative goes beyond this to also probe the *psychological* impact on activists of repeated personal loss. In A *Taste*, Brown paints a portrait of Erica Huggins following her husband John's assassination that offers a poignant illustration of the impact of loss. Although Brown's illustration here is of another's grief rather than her own, the portrait attests to activists' emotional vulnerability in ways not readily exposed by the other women autobiographers. Brown notes that in the immediate aftermath of John's death, Huggins appeared very strong. The determination to cling to righteous anger (like that evident in Shakur's poems) in the face of repeated loss is, after all, a necessary survival strategy making possible individual perseverance and also the advancement of the collective struggle. However, Brown eventually begins to notice changes in Huggins, which she describes as Ericka's apparent "loss of passion," following her release from prison. In the hours following her husband's death, Ericka Huggins was arrested along with Bobby Seale on charges of attempted retaliatory homicide. Whether as a result of John's assassination or of the seventeen months afterward that Huggins spent in solitary confinement before she was acquitted, Brown contends: "her emotional fire was surely gone . . . and I found myself more and more frustrated by that. It seemed to take something away from all of us, especially me" (A *Taste*, 408). Although Brown does not explain what she means in referring to herself as "especially" affected by Huggins's alleged change, it is possible that she is referring back to the way in which the

Party fulfilled her longing for a sense of meaning, purpose, and identity, and by extension to the need for her faith in its righteousness to remain intact. Brown remarks: "The truth was her unburdened sorrow had begun to heighten my sense of doom" (434). It is as if connecting with Huggins's loss—and possibly, her sense of despair—too closely (like Brown's fear later of identifying too closely with the victims of Huey Newton's violent purges of Party activists) could force Brown into an uncomfortable confrontation with everything to which she had up to that point devoted her life. If so, such identification might have threatened to plunge her into the kind of meaninglessness that she spends much of the narrative longing to escape. While Brown claims that she and Huggins were close comrades for nearly ten years, she neglects to speculate on the causes of Huggins's apparent change. Huggins seems the mirror into which Brown is unprepared to look. The glimpse Brown allows of Huggins's alleged change during her incarceration hints at the trauma and impact of loss for activists, the pain that must be kept to the margin.

In addition to the silences in Davis's and Shakur's autobiographies surrounding their personal, interior lives (in contrast to Brown's revelations about the same), their texts also withhold other kinds of information, especially that which might undermine the image of the Movement or imperil the welfare of other activists. Such silences function strategically in each woman's overall political objective. Both Davis and Shakur decline on several occasions, for instance, to mention names of people who supported or assisted them along the way, since such information could easily facilitate retaliation. Davis resists divulging the names of the guards working at the Women's House of Detention who were supportive of her while she was there. As she acknowledges, printing their names in her text at the time could have resulted in their losing their jobs (*Autobiography*, 43). Similarly, Shakur says of the individuals who supported her: "I would mention their names, but the way things are today, i'd only be sending the FBI or CIA to their doors" (*Assata*, 189). Her comment anticipates her readers' curiosity, particularly with regard to the details of her escape from prison, but also presumes her readers' understanding. Astutely, she accounts for the reality of both hostile and sympathetic audiences. Most importantly, her silence in such instances, like Davis's, is intended to protect the interests and integrity of the

Movement in a way that also leaves space for other activists to benefit from the kinds of opportunities made available to her.

In contrast to Brown's narrative, which occasionally includes details of specific missions (such as her rendezvous with John Huggins to carry out an act of guerilla warfare—*A Taste*, 154), Shakur avoids recounting her own involvement in clandestine activities. Instead, her narrative, like Davis's, is concerned largely with defending herself against bogus charges for crimes she did not commit. Whether there were other crimes she *did* commit in the course of her activist work remains notably vague, and—since political autobiography is in major part concerned with redefining criminality (by challenging a status quo that overwhelmingly favors the interests of a capitalist elite at the expense of all others)—even inconsequential. Although Shakur refers repeatedly to her participation in various community and campus political protests and demonstrations in New York City (*Assata*, 204), her involvement in the antiwar movement, her association with the Harlem branch of the Black Panther Party, and later her underground involvement with the Black Liberation Army, surprisingly the most subtle silence in Shakur's text is that surrounding details of her actual activities as a revolutionary. It is a subtle silence because her status and identity as a revolutionary is already overdetermined by the fact of the narrative itself. It is, after all, the basis of the authority from which she speaks, and the condition we, as readers, are led to take for granted. At one point, Shakur indicates that she was prepared to join the Panthers but postponed her affiliation for reasons that remain ambiguous in her account. Enigmatically, she explains: "i had some other things i wanted to do and i needed a low profile in order to do them" (204). What these "other things" are is never revealed. Later, on learning about a series of killings of policemen, she indicates that she was shocked by the news and yet awed that "somebody was finally doing what the rest of us merely had fantasies about" (236). Shortly after this news, however, she learns from an article in the paper that she herself is wanted "for questioning" in association with the killings. Shakur is thus forced underground into hiding in the same way that Davis was after the Marin County courtroom siege.

If the silences around Shakur's *particular* activities can be described as subtle, then the silences surrounding details of her prison escape are commensurately glaring. Although Shakur's release is foreshadowed by a vision her grandmother relays, an ellipsis stands in for details of the actual escape. Shakur offers only a veiled reference to her own agency by explaining that once her grandmother prophesied things, it was the responsibility of those concerned to make the dream come true (260). The most potentially climactic moment in *Assata* (Shakur builds narrative tension by alluding to her own increasing restlessness and anxiety behind bars) is thus rendered anticlimactic by analepsis (261). In place of the details of her escape (e.g., when, under what conditions, and by what means), we are instead offered her first impressions of freedom as she seeks exile in Cuba (266). Only by recourse to secondary materials is some of the enigma dispelled. In "Self-Portrait of a Black Liberationist: An Appraisal of Assata Shakur's Autobiography," M. Annette Jaimes, for instance, indicates that Shakur was smuggled from the maximum-security building of New Jersey's Clinton Prison for Women on November 2, 1979, by members of the Revolutionary Armed Task Force, a wing of the Black Liberation Army (Churchill and Vander Wall, *Cages*, 242). Another source offering a little more detail describes how she was rescued after "three male visitors drew handguns, kidnapped two guards and seized a prison minibus in order to drive out of the grounds to two getaway cars." The source notes that the guards were left "handcuffed but unharmed," and also that the men involved were assisted by another woman (Kihss). Clearly, both silences (the first surrounding Shakur's specific activities as a revolutionary, and the second her startling escape from prison) are strategic, since the implications of her disclosures necessarily extend beyond her text. Such silences emphasize the inseparability of political autobiography from its social and political context.

Such strategic silences in Shakur's and Davis's narratives are a reflection of the kind of text each envisioned herself writing (i.e., one that would be an extension of her continuing struggle) as well as the sociopolitical context in which each text emerged. Brown, writing in a different era, is less concerned (and has more freedom to be so) with upholding Party propaganda or promoting positive images of the Movement than with illuminating the points at which both sometimes went wrong. In an interview with Renée Graham for the *Boston Globe*, Brown insists: "I didn't want to write a chronicle of the Black Panther Party. I wanted to write a chronicle of a black woman's life" (Graham, 32).

Angela Davis, in a generally favorable review of A *Taste*, concedes that the book is less a history of the Party than an exposé of one woman's experience in that party—her "relations with the Party's men, ideas, disciplines and projects" (Davis, "The Making," 4). The story of the Party's relation to the larger culture is thus subjugated in A *Taste* to the story of Party members' relationships to each other, and, if one accepts fellow Black Panther Kathleen Cleaver's criticism in "Sister Act: Symbol and Substance in Black Women's Leadership," to the story of Brown's involvement with Huey Newton in particular (Cleaver, 96). Because A *Taste* addresses such issues as internecine violence, sexism, and misogyny within the Movement, Davis proposed that the book "would have been inconceivable in the seventies—or even the eighties. In radical circles, it would have been considered tantamount to treason, and among conservatives it would have been welcomed as the exposé of a fraudulent movement" (Davis, "The Making," 4). Brown's focus on the internal politics and affairs of the Black Panther Party and on her own experiences negotiating within the Party's ruling elite subsumes concern over the political terrain outside the organization, and consequently marks her text as engaged in a different kind of political work. While Brown's transgressing of certain personal and strategic silences sets her text apart from Davis's and Shakur's, this move also makes worthwhile our reading her text alongside theirs. That is, Brown supplies information that, in many ways, complements Davis's and Shakur's accounts, and that, in the process, gives us greater insight into the forms and substance of Black female radicalism during the period. The noteworthy differences between their texts notwithstanding, what Brown's, Shakur's, and Davis's autobiographies share in common connects their works and lives to a formidable tradition of African American resistance writing and struggle.

Chapter 2

Literary Antecedents in the Struggle for Freedom

The history of African American writing bears witness not only to the experience of oppression, but just as importantly, to a continuum of individual and collective resistance. This continuum, or movement toward liberation, has always consisted of many different impulses. Historian Vincent Harding used the metaphor of a river with many currents to symbolize the diverse ideologies informing African American resistance struggle from the eighteenth through the nineteenth century. In *There Is a River: The Black Struggle for Freedom in America*, Harding argued that by the beginning of the eighteenth century, "many basic currents in the black river" were in place. Moving from the surface to the deepest level, Harding identified the emergence of three major currents: *survival* (e.g., myriad forms of subterfuge, passing, subversive humor, guile, artistic expression), *protest and resistance* (e.g., work slowdowns, destruction of labor equipment, civil disobedience, flight), and *radicalism* (e.g., forms of revolutionary struggle, including armed revolt) (Harding, 51). In the course of his study, Harding placed the names of well-known and lesser-known African American activists within the currents of protest and resistance and of radicalism. Within the former, which he also described as the "Great Tradition of Protest," one finds the work and ideas of such prominent individuals as Frederick Douglass, Henry Highland Garnet, Harriet Tubman, and Sojourner Truth. If one were to extend the scope of Harding's study (which culminates in the period of Reconstruction), such figures as Martin Luther King Jr., Ella Baker, Septima Clark, and other activists of the Civil Rights Movement might also be added. By contrast, Harding placed within the radical ideological current such historical figures as David Walker, Nat Turner, Denmark Vesey, and (the early) Martin Delaney. Again, extending his definition into the more contemporary context, one might add the names of Malcolm X, Huey Newton, Assata Shakur, Stokely Carmichael, Angela Davis, David Hilliard, and Elaine Brown, as well as other activists of the Black Power Movement.

The ideological currents Harding describes are evident not only in the sociopolitical arena, but also in the vast body of African American literature, both fiction and nonfiction. And while this literature cannot be reduced solely to themes of invisibility, inequity, powerlessness, disenfranchisement, and persecution (along with evidence of resistance to and triumph over these phenomena), these are recurring themes throughout the body of literature by African American writers. Arguably, in exploring such themes, one finds that much of African American writing is *explicitly* political. When Harding's terms are translated into the realm of African American literary history, much of African American literature, from the slave (or as critic Eleanor Traylor more aptly puts it, *emancipation*) narratives through the contemporary period, can be thematically situated along the currents of survival, protest and resistance, and radicalism.

As activists of the Black Power Movement committed to revolutionary struggle against capitalist and racist oppression, Angela Davis, Assata Shakur, and Elaine Brown exemplify a radical current in African American political resistance. Their individual and collective commitment to revolutionary activism is evident in the kind of autobiography each produces. Like other leftist radicals, Davis, Shakur, and Brown seek through their work (as both activists and writers) to alter mass consciousness by disrupting the status quo in a way they believe will lead to progressive social transformation. Although their texts, based on this criterion, might conceivably be discussed alongside the autobiographical works of such other twentieth-century African American activist writers as Richard Wright, James Baldwin, and Audre Lorde, their texts are also distinct from such works on several accounts. First, none of the women identifies primarily as a literary figure. Second, Davis's, Shakur's and Brown's narratives are marked by each author's immersion—either prior to or at the time of writing—in organized political struggle (i.e., apart from individual/personal acts of resistance). Third, their texts, like the emancipation narratives, are meant to bear witness to a reality beyond their own personal circumstances. Finally, their autobiographies are additionally distinguished by each writer's precarious status vis-à-vis mainstream society and the law, *and* their autobiographical focus on this particular aspect of their lives. For these reasons, Angela Davis's term, "political autobiography," becomes a particularly useful way of naming the distinction between activists' texts like hers and the larger body of twentieth-century African American autobiography. In the preface to her narrative, Davis explains that she deliberately set out to write a *political autobiography*: "When I decided to write the book after all, it was because I had come to envision it as a political autobiography that emphasized the people, the events and the forces in my life that propelled me to my present commitment" (*Autobiography*, xvi). She also notes that she wrote with two primary objectives: first, to raise the consciousness of readers by helping them better understand the particular conditions that necessitated resistance struggle by African Americans and other oppressed groups; and second, to encourage others to join the struggle. She elaborates: "In this period . . . there was the possibility that more people— Black, Brown, Red, Yellow and white—might be inspired to join our growing community of struggle. Only if this happens will I consider this project to have been worthwhile" (xvi). In offering their lives as example, activists demonstrate the potential for individuals to actively transform their material conditions. In this way, their autobiographies offer readers models of what radical educator Henry Giroux has termed "insurgent subjectivity" (*Disturbing Pleasures*, 62).

Importantly, the women's narratives testify not only to their experiences of oppression, but also to the extent to which such experiences are tied to systemic phenomena. In this way, their texts are engaged with theorizing personal experience. In differentiating theoretical writing from other forms of expository writing, Houston Baker observes that theoretical writing is marked by its "relentless tendency . . . to go beyond the tangible in search of metalevels of explanation" (Baker, 38). In the case of all three women's narratives, life experiences involving racism, sexism, and economic exploitation, for example, are frequently interrogated in order to expose and explore their structural causes. Nevertheless, given the sense in which the term is most often invoked within the academy, some critics (ironically, including Baker himself) might argue that Davis's, Shakur's, and Brown's texts are *not* theoretical. As Carole Boyce Davies, Barbara Christian, and others have argued, however, such a claim presupposes a very narrow definition of what it means to do theory. Certainly, a great deal of theorizing takes place in texts not necessarily marked as "theoretical." Paraphrasing the work of Catherine Lutz, Carole Boyce Davies, in *Black Women, Writing and Identity: Migrations of the Subject*, enumerates the ways in which writing is conventionally identified and legitimated as theory within academic discourse. She contends: "theory signals itself in certain ways—first, through self-labeling, second, abstract language, identified with levels of difficulty, third, styles and modes of citation of others' work . . . and fourth, the text's positioning of itself at, or in relation to, a moment of origin" (Davies, 39).[1] The reason such a definition of what it means to do theory is narrow is that it presupposes that theoretical insight is inextricably bound to one particular type or method of writing. In reality, the practice of theorizing takes place in many different forms and contexts. Theory is, foremost, an act of translation ostensibly motivated by the will to make meaning. To engage in theory, by this definition, is to propose ways of conceptualizing or understanding that serve to demystify or clarify experience. In the broadest sense, then, theoretical language includes that which analyzes by explaining how and why, that which illuminates cause-and-effect relationships, and that which exposes connections between divers and/or disparate phenomena. Writing that is theoretical probes beneath surfaces to discover and articulate meaning not readily apparent. Because many different kinds of writing (as well as speech) are engaged in various ways with this fundamental project, limiting what it means to do theory to a particular type of academic writing is at best exclusive, and at worst tragic, since the implication is that we can only learn something valuable (about Black women's lives, for instance) from a privileged minority who have access to this language. In arguing for theoretical dimensions to Davis's, Brown's, and Shakur's writing, I am also arguing for a broader appreciation of the myriad contexts and voices in which theoretical insights can be (and are) articulated.

In theorizing their own experiences, activist autobiographers seek to

---

[1] Davies cites an unpublished manuscript by Lutz, "The Gender of Theory" (1990). The last criterion Davies mentions—i.e., "the text's positioning of itself at, or in relation to, a moment of origin"—refers to a text's offering itself as a new/original way of entering, conceptualizing, or explaining a given phenomenon.

alter the consciousness of their readers. Their narratives address crucial omissions in the historical record and endeavor to destabilize dominant ways of knowing by openly challenging hegemonic assumptions. The radical significance of activists' texts is in how their words compel readers to grapple with the sociopolitical landscape *outside* of the text. This imperative is a salient feature of resistance literature. In defining resistance literature, critic Barbara Harlow has noted the way such writing "calls attention to itself, and to literature in general, as a political and politicized activity. The literature of resistance sees itself furthermore as immediately and directly involved in a struggle against ascendant or dominant forms of ideological and cultural production" (Harlow, *Resistance*, 28). Harlow's definition clearly situates resistance literature within a sociopolitical and historical context that challenges the apolitical bent of New Critical approaches to literary study. The autobiographies of political activists deconstruct, as Harlow also has argued, "the very institution of literature as an autonomous arena of activity" (Harlow, *Barred*, 4). As a site of both ideology and pedagogy, literature is always inextricably bound to past or present political struggle. Treating activists' works critically and responsibly entails by necessity more than an aesthetic valuation of the writing. Some engagement with the kinds of political issues activists' stories address is also incumbent. In addition to agitating for critical literacy that leads to practice, their works suggest new ways of envisioning literary study. That is, it becomes important that we study literature not just as a repository of culture, but also as a pedagogical resource in the work of *transforming* culture.

The autobiographical form is particularly suited to activists' objectives. Given the popularity the genre enjoys in the United States alone, autobiography presents activists with an opportunity to engage a potentially broad audience in their work and ideas. Furthermore, autobiography's affinity to multiple fields of study besides literature (e.g., history, sociology, psychology, ethnic and gender studies) additionally affords their narratives opportunities for continued recuperation from potential obscurity. As critic Albert Stone once noted: "*Life* is the more inclusive sign—not *Literature*—which deserves to be placed above the gateway to the house of autobiography" (Stone, 19). It is no coincidence, then, that there is a long history of African American activists writing autobiography.

Indeed, conventions common to Davis's, Shakur's, and Brown's autobiographies invite us to situate their texts along a continuum of African American resistance writing that begins with the emancipation narratives. As with these early activist-writers, Davis's, Shakur's, and Brown's testimony is valued not only for what they say about their own lives, but for their witnessing of events beyond their immediate circumstances. Robert Stepto argues that because the emancipation narrators tended to write in the voice of participant-observers, calling their texts "autobiographical" is almost a misnomer (Stepto, 16). A similar argument could be made on behalf of many of the Black Power autobiographers in the sense that their stories are the witnessing not only of their own circumstances, but of a reality shared by many others as well. Like the emancipation narrators who were expected to write as witnesses to the experiences of slavery in general, recent authors of political autobiography tend to subordinate the uniqueness of their own experience to the way in which it reflects the shared reality of many. Henry Louis Gates Jr. notes that because the emancipation narrators tended to familiarize themselves with the writing of fellow slaves, this also influenced the quality of their testimony. He argues that, in the process of imitation and repetition, "the black slave's narrative came to be a communal utterance, a collective tale, rather than merely an individual's autobiography. Each slave author, in writing about his or her personal life's experiences, simultaneously wrote on behalf of millions of silent slaves still held captive throughout the South" (Gates, x). The fact that Davis, Shakur, and Brown incorporate into their narratives multiple allusions to the condition of slavery thematically ties their autobiographies to the emancipation narratives and also reveals the extent to which they self-consciously and strategically link their own experiences to those of earlier activists. It is probable that all three women would have been familiar with Frederick Douglass's *Narrative of the Life* (1845), and that Shakur and Brown at least may also have known of Harriet Jacobs's *Incidents in the Life of a Slave Girl*. I mention Douglass and Jacobs in particular because their texts have enjoyed considerable popularity over the past several years. Both have additionally received extensive critical attention as complementary studies for theorizing differences between masculine and feminine paradigms of resistance struggle. In her introduction to the 1987 reprint of *Incidents in the Life of a Slave Girl* (1861), editor Jean

Fagan Yellin indicates that, although Jacobs's achievement was not fully recognized until "the accession of her letters in the Post Archive at the University of Rochester made it possible in 1981 to authenticate her authorship," her story was republished and circulated along with several other slave narratives during the height of the Civil Rights Movement (Jacobs, xvi). However, even had Davis, Shakur, and Brown not read these or other such texts, their experiences under racist oppression, as well as their participation in African American collective consciousness, would have been sufficient to create noteworthy parallels between their texts and those of their forebears.

Themes and motifs traceable from the emancipation narratives through the works by Davis, Shakur, and Brown are numerous. Like their antecedents, all three women address the struggle for literacy and the commitment to self-education it necessarily entails. For the emancipation narrators as well as for more recent activist writers like the three studied here, literacy is tied to freedom. As Gates notes: "the slave who learned to read and write was the first to run away" (Gates, ix). Not only does the ability to read and write facilitate individual physical and psychic liberation, it also opens up the possibility for amassing an audience. During a period when both Davis and Shakur were extremely vulnerable to political neutralization and/or detention stemming from their activities, for example, their writing an autobiography was a useful means of protecting themselves from renewed harassment and persecution. Davis was in prison when she began penning her autobiography, while Shakur was (and remains) a wanted fugitive. In making the public at least aware of their predicament, they endeavored to amass potential support and also to undermine the ability of the state to retaliate against them in secrecy. All three women thus share with the emancipation narrators the project not only of writing their lives, but—to different degrees—of *writing for their lives.*

In a society that privileges and venerates the written word (over oral testimony), marginalized groups have recognized historically the importance of literacy; writing is the primary means by which a public voice—a voice capable of being heard beyond one's immediate community—is acquired. Of course, writing does not necessarily mean that one's words *will* be heard, only that one's words are *eligible* to be heard. Writing, in a logocentric culture, is furthermore the primary means of giving legitimacy not only to ideas, but also to human beings. Shakur comments ironically in her narrative, for example, on the way the authorities' inability to locate her birth records calls her very existence into question. She begins chapter 2: "The FBI cannot find any evidence that i was born" (*Assata*, 18). Her statement signifies on the absurdity of a situation in which papers legitimize *human beings* rather than the other way around. Defying the prospect of bureaucratic erasure, she declares satirically: "Anyway, i was born." (The gesture parallels later instances in the narrative where she challenges the notion of "official history" as the only way of knowing.) Since writing functions to preserve, there is always the advantage that one's words may be recovered or heard anew long after their original utterance. By contrast, those who have no access to the privileged domain of influence, where ideas turn into policies that are debated and disseminated (e.g., the universities and corporate board rooms of America), are ultimately consigned to silence no matter how aggressively or how consistently they speak. It is this understanding that motivates activists who write their stories to speak not just in the interests of the personal "I," but on behalf of countless others who may never have access to this privileged arena.

Importantly, however, Davis's, Shakur's, and Brown's narratives also revise the meaning of literacy as it was understood by the emancipation narrators. Whereas functional literacy was paramount for the emancipation narrators, Black Power activists' autobiographies collectively reveal a distinct shift in focus from the value of functional literacy alone to the importance of cultivating critical or, as Paulo Freire argues in *The Politics of Education, political* literacy as the prerequisite to self-empowerment. In both instances, the knowledge sought is subversive to the extent that oppressed people who acquire literacy almost always cease to be content. Critical/political literacy differs from functional literacy in that it names the capacity to interpret social reality based on an analysis of power relations and an awareness of history. Shakur, for example, states that "to win any struggle for liberation, you have to have the way as well as the will, an overall ideology and strategy that stem from a scientific analysis of history and present conditions" (*Assata*, 242). The attention to critical literacy that characterizes Davis's, Shakur's, and Brown's narratives contributes to the pedagogical value of their texts. All recognize the Black Power resistance struggle as part of a much larger movement.

They link the struggle of African Americans not only with other indigenous struggles (that is, of American Indians, Chicanos/as, and Asian Americans), but also with the various liberation struggles being waged abroad by people of color against imperialist exploitation and oppression. As H. Bruce Franklin notes: "in the epic of worldwide national liberation struggles, the Afro-American vision moves from the understanding of being colonial victim to a sense of national—and international—war against colonial enslavement" (Franklin, 247). All three women have both access to a vast body of political ideology and theory, including revolutionary writings by such figures as Marx, Nkrumah, Nyere, Mao, and Guevara, and the benefit of insight gained from the Cuban revolution as well as the various independence struggles that were being waged on the African continent. Having studied other political systems, all three writers are able to interrogate capitalist ideology and practice as a source of mass suffering.

Through the act of writing, Black Power activists, like their forebears, endeavor not only to validate their own experiences, but also to recreate themselves against disparaging definitions and negative images imposed on them by a racist and sexist culture. In general the autobiographers of the Black Power Movement are less concerned than the emancipation narrators were with writing in order to prove their humanity. Anticipating an appreciable Black as well as White readership, none of their works is fashioned primarily as an appeal to the moral conscience of Whites. A major thrust of the Black Power Movement, in fact, was that the imperative for social change could not, should not, and would not any longer wait on Whites to be convinced of the moral right of oppressed people to struggle against their oppression. The appeal to Christian morality that is a prominent feature of the emancipation narratives is thus conspicuously absent in these later narratives.

While Black Power activists are not particularly concerned, then, with writing to prove their humanity, writing autobiography nevertheless provides them an opportunity to refashion an identity against disparaging images of themselves propagated in the popular press. Shakur, for example, describes the way she was vilified and victimized in the media by racist myths of Black monstrosity. She refers specifically to the publication of Robert Daley's *Target Blue*, which became a major source of information for the press in reporting on her. At the time, Daley was the deputy commissioner of the New York City police department in charge of public relations. Excerpts from his book appeared as an article in the February 12, 1973, edition of the *New York Magazine* (Williams, 6, 125). In the wake of this propaganda, Shakur remarks how those who met her in person were often astounded by her surprisingly diminutive stature (about 5′6″). She recalls: "Everybody told me they thought i was bigger, blacker, and uglier. When i asked people what they thought i looked like, they would describe someone about six feet tall, two hundred pounds, and very dark and wild-looking" (*Assata*, 87). For members of oppressed groups in general, this objective of autobiography to "re-write the self" is particularly resonant since, as Janice Morgan has argued, "to be marginalized to a dominant culture is also to have had little or no say in the construction of one's socially acknowledged identity" (Morgan and Hall, xv). The act of writing the self frequently constitutes a move from invisibility to visibility (after all, to be seen for something other than who one is is still to exist in a state of invisibility). In *De/Colonizing the Subject: The Politics of Gender in Women's Autobiography*, editors Sidonie Smith and Julia Watson propose that "for the marginalized woman, autobiographical language may serve as a coinage that purchases entry into the social and discursive economy" (Smith and Watson, xix). That is, personal experience functions as an important knowledge base from which to speak. The "I" of autobiographical writing facilitates (at least discursively) the move from passive object (of others' discourses) to active subject. In the process, the autobiographer also establishes herself as the authority over her own experiences. One might add that Smith and Watson's claim on behalf of women writers holds true for other marginalized groups as well.

Apart from the quest for literacy and the move toward subjectivity, a third issue joining the narratives by Davis, Shakur, and Brown to those by the emancipation narrators is the experience of displacement/cultural alienation and the search for community once the individual is severed from his or her birth community. Quite often, the consequence of gaining literacy or critical consciousness is alienation not just from the values of the dominant culture, but from the ways of knowing and being that characterize one's own immediate family and community. The quest for freedom thus necessitates finding new communities of support among those who share or are at least receptive to similar values. Finally and perhaps most strikingly, the Black Power autobiographers share with the emancipation narrators the experience of violence. In some instances this violence is literal (as in poverty/material deprivation, hunger, physical assault, murder, rape/sexual assault, and torture), while in others it is figurative (involving, for example, the experience of erasure/invisibility or of learned self-hatred).

Not insignificantly, both Davis and Shakur are fugitives as their narratives open. Wanted by the FBI in connection with a shootout at the Marin County Courthouse, Davis fled underground to avoid capture. By that time, she had already endured extensive political harassment (including dismissal from her job) because of her avowed membership in the Communist Party. Explaining her decision to go underground, Davis writes that: "No one needed to tell me that they would exploit the fact that my guns had been used in Marin in order to strike out at me once more" (*Autobiography*, 6). Self-consciously situating herself within a historical continuum of African American resistance, Davis describes her flight underground to evade capture by the police: "Thousands of my ancestors had waited, as I had done, for nightfall to cover their steps, had leaned on one true friend to help them, had felt, as I did, the very teeth of the dogs at their heels" (6). Davis's imagery clearly evokes the slave fleeing the plantation. Also like runaway slaves, both Shakur and Davis resort to disguise to maintain mobility while underground. Bettina Aptheker, who became part of Davis's legal defense team, notes further that when Davis was finally arraigned, it was on charges of violating the Federal Interstate Fugitive Act, "a direct descendant of the Fugitive Slave Law" (Aptheker, 110). Fugitive slave laws were enacted in 1793 and 1850; both statutes had provisions for fugitives from the law as well as fugitives from labor (i.e., slavery). When Davis regained her freedom after being acquitted of the charges against her, she took up the tradition of Harriet Tubman by continuing to organize for the freedom of other political prisoners.

Shakur's description of her eventual escape from prison, like Davis's description of her flight underground, is also noteworthy for the way it parallels the escapes described in the narratives of both Frederick Douglass and Harriet Jacobs. That Shakur's daughter becomes the motivation for her escape is notably reminiscent of Jacobs's experience. Like Douglass's and Jacobs's flight from bondage, Shakur's escape from prison takes place underground; therefore, details which might jeopardize the opportunity for others in the future to escape by similar means are omitted from her narrative. Unlike Douglass and Jacobs, who find refuge in traveling north (a place Shakur would not have been safe from extradition), however, Shakur flees south, where she is granted asylum in Cuba.

In *Prison Literature in America: The Victim As Criminal and Artist,* H. Bruce Franklin draws a parallel between the way Douglass's narrative endeavors to show how slavery turns a man into a beast and the way contemporary resistance narratives show how American capitalist oppression turns citizens into criminals. Summarizing Douglass's conclusion, Franklin asserts that consciousness is what "allows people to alter the conditions of existence, a consciousness that develops in the struggle for freedom from brute necessity" (Franklin, 18). In a sentiment that seems to echo Douglass perfectly, Shakur declares: "The less you think about your oppression, the more your tolerance for it grows. After a while, people just think oppression is the normal state of things. But to become free, you have to be acutely aware of being a slave" (*Assata,* 262). The narratives of Davis, Shakur, and Brown all chronicle changing consciousness leading to revolutionary struggle.

One of the most striking parallels to the condition of slavery is what these three women write about the experiences of police detention and incarceration. The combination of physical abuse and mental torture (prisons seek foremost to break the spirit of political prisoners), the use of shackling, the reality of constant surveillance, the exploitation of inmate labor, the enforced separation of mothers and their children, and other human rights abuses suggest clear parallels between the prison system and the institution of chattel slavery. Shakur, in fact, makes the parallel explicit, noting that the labor of prisoners can be exacted legally (under the Thirteenth Amendment to the Constitution) without remuneration.

There is a clear parallel between the vulnerability slaves experienced in captivity and the vulnerability contemporary political prisoners endure in detention. In the emancipation narratives as well as the narratives by Black Power activists, the fear for physical safety against the constant threat of bodily harm is something experienced by both women and men. Davis, Shakur, and Brown all describe the reality of their physical/sexual vulnerability while in police custody. Davis relates a particularly tense moment in custody during her extradition from New York to California to stand trial. Like Shakur, who writes that her "abrupt transfer from one jail to another, without either notice to [her] lawyers or explanation to [her], was a scenario that would be repeated over and over again" (*Assata*, 80), Davis describes being moved swiftly without advance notice or indication of where she was being taken. In the process of being transferred, she also is made acutely aware of her own dispensability. Surrounded by agents poised to shoot at the slightest provocation, she is sobered by the realization that if she even so much as tripped in her approach to the waiting aircraft, she could easily be killed. She writes: "their attack reflexes would be set off. And my body would be riddled with bullets. Since this operation was being conducted in secrecy, away from the eyes of the press, there would be no one to contradict them if they said I was trying to escape" (*Autobiography*, 72).

The excessive display of force associated with Shakur's transport from New Jersey to New York to stand trial parallels Davis's experience. The absurdity of the situation is emphasized by Shakur's almost comical rendering of the chain of events. In addition to the procession consisting of about twelve cars flanking the one in which she was riding, Shakur notes that a New Jersey state patrol car had been positioned at every exit along the Turnpike. She elaborates: "All the cars had lights on and sirens going. A helicopter trailed us. And the pigs in the car i was in were comical. At every point they said something like 'At least we got to the turnpike.' 'At least we got to the bridge.' 'At least we got to New York.' 'At least we made it to the court.' . . . They acted like they were on some dangerous mission inside Russia. They were actually afraid" (*Assata*, 65). Shakur situates this fear in the context of Black-White relations historically. According to Shakur, the White policemen act less out of any realistic assessment of the immediate circumstances than out of presumption and fear of anticipated reprisal for past wrongdoing. Both Shakur's and Davis's accounts reveal the extent to which they are victimized by the culture's myths of Black monstrosity. Even when shackled, each is treated as if she had some sort of superhuman powers that would enable her to violently overpower her captors and escape. This point is underscored by Shakur's detailed description of the extent to which prisoners in transport are restrained. She writes: "First [the marshal] shackles my feet; then he puts a chain around my waist, fastens the handcuffs to the chain, and handcuffs on my hands. I can barely walk. Or shuffle" (88).

In more than one confrontation with the police, Brown describes similar fears of being murdered by racist officers whose abuses of power and trigger-happy tendencies in confronting Black activists could be easily dismissed by pleas of self-defense or "justifiable homicide." Brown relates the sense of terror and helplessness in confrontations in which cops produced nonstandard issue firearms and in which the slightest unauthorized move could result in death. Brown further notes that it was not uncommon for male police officers to violate the law by conducting body searches of female suspects (A Taste, 182). In her description of the first time she was detained, Brown recounts the particular type of degrading sexist abuse to which she was subjected. She writes: " 'You're the oldest whore of the pink pussies [a reference to Brown's former employment at the Pink Pussycat nightclub],' they said to me on the ride to the 77th Precinct, 'so you must be the one with the biggest hole' " (169). For Shakur the threat of physical harm in detention is even more ominous, both because of the particular charges against her (she is accused of shooting a state trooper) and the length of time she spends incarcerated. In contrast to the years Shakur spends behind bars, Brown, for instance, appears to spend only a few days in the Sybil Brand Institute (county jail) before charges against her are ultimately dropped (169).

In her autobiography, Shakur retells a particularly harrowing experience in which she is awakened one night by the surprise appearance of several unauthorized male guards in the doorway to her cell. She is saved from potential harm only by the clatter of the metal cups she had strategically stacked at the entrance to alert her (and presumably others as well) to intruders. No longer able to covertly carry out their intended mission (which could have entailed anything from rape and/or battery to attempted murder), the guards eventually retreat. Like Brown, Shakur conveys the sense in which being labeled as an outlaw means that one's safety and welfare also fall outside any protection from the law; violent assaults on prisoners, like those on slaves, are generally committed with impunity. She advises: "In prisons, it is not at all uncommon to find a prisoner hanged or burned to death in his cell. No matter how suspicious the circumstances, these deaths are always ruled 'suicides.' They are usually Black inmates, considered to be a 'threat to the orderly running of the prison' " (*Assata*, 59). Shakur further notes that the victims of these alleged "suicides" tend to be the "most politically aware and socially conscious inmates in prison."

As Brown's, Shakur's and Davis's narratives repeatedly attest, the treatment received by women in custody or detention is scarcely distinguishable from that received by men in terms of the potential brutality of their respective captors. Shakur's narrative, in fact, opens dramatically with the description of her violent capture on the New Jersey Turnpike. She recounts first the sensation of having been shot, and then the aggravation of her already precarious condition—the extent of her injuries including a bullet wound to the chest, an injured lung, a broken clavicle, and a paralyzed arm (17)—by further police aggression. She writes: "Suddenly the [car] door flew open and i felt myself being dragged out onto the pavement. Pushed and punched, a foot upside my head, a kick in the stomach. Police were everywhere. One had a gun to my head. 'Which way did they go,' he was shouting. 'Bitch, you'd better open your goddamn mouth or I'll blow your goddamn head off!' " (3). Shakur's vulnerability continues during her hospital stay in police custody. In the hospital, her welfare remains precarious while she is held incommunicado from the outside world. She is additionally denied adequate medical attention. Augmenting her torture, the attending medical staff decline to discuss with her the extent or implications of her injuries. Her hospital room becomes a site of around-the-clock interrogation, harassment, and torture, which is alleviated only periodically by the entrance of sympathetic nursing staff. The law enforcement officers attending her bedside become her trial by jury long before she is officially charged with any crime. Like the civil rights activists who strategically resorted to song to alter and reclaim space from their persecutors, Shakur creates a counter-discourse to the verbal abuse of her tormentors by reciting resistance poetry aloud (16).

In the autobiographies of Black Power activists, as in the emancipation narratives, one finds a constant stripping and reinscribing of femininity and masculinity in ways intended to humiliate and degrade captive subjects. In this regard alone, the parallel between the predicament of Davis, Shakur, and Brown in captivity to that of enslaved African women historically is noteworthy. In her book *Women, Race, and Class*, Angela Davis maintains that "[e]xpediency governed the slaveholder's posture toward female slaves: when it was profitable to exploit them as if they were men, they were regarded, in effect, as genderless, but when they could be exploited, punished and repressed in ways suited only for women, they were locked into their exclusively female roles" (Davis, *Women*, 6). This meant that Black women were regarded primarily as exploitable and expendable labor subject to the same intensity of violence as Black men. Although there are some qualitative differences that do emerge relative to gender, the experiences of women and men activists in captivity resemble each other more than they diverge. Shakur's retelling of beatings she received in police custody surely undermines the myth that Black women receive any sort of leniency with respect to physical abuse in detention. On one occasion Shakur is beaten in court when she refuses to be photographed following the judge's order. Her refusal stems from a legitimate concern that the photo might be altered/manipulated by the FBI to match a video image. The "match" could then be used to secure her conviction in a bank robbery charge. As a result of her refusal, Shakur indicates that she was beaten, choked, and kicked by five marshals, even as her lawyer narrated each blow into the court record (*Assata*, 161). On yet another occasion, she describes being beaten and restrained by several large female officers upon refusing a medical exam from the prison physician shortly after giving birth (144). Shakur maintains that her own situation was not unique in this regard. Referring to her stay in the Middlesex County Jail, she writes that "it was nothing to see a woman brought in all beat up" (54). She recalls, for example, a Puerto Rican woman who arrived so badly beaten by the police that the matron on duty was reluctant to admit her for fear that the woman might die on her shift. Through her acquaintance with Eva (a fellow inmate at Middlesex), Shakur learns of similar incidents involving other women. Eva, for instance, relays that when she was at the Clinton Correctional facility for women in New Jersey, she witnessed a pregnant woman beaten so viciously that the woman miscarried (60).

Interestingly, Black women and Black men both report a psychosexual dimension to the abuse they receive under White prison staff while in detention. Women, in addition to being beaten or maimed, can also expect to be raped. While men may be less susceptible to the particular crime of rape by the police, a sexual dimension nevertheless pertains in the kind of abuse they experience in captivity. In *Soledad Brother*, George Jackson refers to the apparent fascination of prison guards with Black men's genitals, noting that "white pigs get a special delight from beating a black around the groin area" (Jackson, *Soledad*, 26). A more recent narrative by Sanyika Shakur (a.k.a. Monster Kody Scott), *Monster: The Autobiography of an L.A. Gang Member*, corroborates Jackson's claim. Shakur writes: "I learned that Americans [Caucasians] have a thing for attacking our private parts during a scuffle. Every incident I've been involved in or witnessed, the private parts of the beatee would be viciously attacked without missing a beat, as if some grudge existed between them and our dicks. Later on I learned that it did" (S. Shakur, 139). Jackson's and Sanyika Shakur's reports are certainly consistent with the long history of psychosexual violence against Black Americans, exemplified perhaps most graphically by the brutal ritual of lynching.

Not only are Black women and men subjected to similar physical abuse in captivity, they also endure similar material conditions. This reality is addressed at length in Davis's autobiography. In the course of corresponding with George Jackson, Davis corrects the prevailing perception—a presumption also held by Jackson—that the conditions inside women's prisons, for example, are fundamentally better than those the men endure. Like Jackson, who insists that racial tension between inmates was continually provoked by the guards, Assata Shakur maintains that when she was transferred to Alderson federal prison in Virginia, she was deliberately placed on a wing disproportionately populated by women who identified themselves as members of the White supremacist Aryan nation, and who were, therefore, openly hostile to her presence. No other women of color were held in that wing. In terms of conditions within the actual prison cells, Davis notes that mice and roaches were constant companions during her incarceration at the House of Detention in New York. In *If They Come in the Morning*, Davis recalls that the women would often "discover roaches cooked into our food." She elaborates: "Not too long ago, a sister found a mousetail in her soup. A few days ago I was drinking a cup of coffee and I was forced to spit out a roach" (Davis, *Morning*, 187). Conditions inside Shakur's Middlesex County Jail basement cell, by comparison, were so revolting that a panel of international jurists representing the United Nations Commission on Human Rights concluded that she was subject to conditions "totally unbefitting any prisoner" (*Assata*, 66). According to Shakur's lawyer, Evelyn Williams, Shakur was exposed to 24-hour surveillance under fluorescent light, a cell infested with insects, a constantly damp cement floor, and leaking overhead pipes. Kept in continual solitary confinement, she was additionally denied opportunities for fresh air, exercise, or communication with either visitors (aside from her attorneys) or other inmates. As if these circumstances were not enough, she was further denied, while pregnant, a nutritionally adequate diet, thus jeopardizing the health and safe delivery of her unborn child (Williams, 126–27).

Life in prison under continual surveillance, the constant threat of violence, and the unrelenting subjection to countless indignities (e.g., strip searches, infantilizing treatment by prison staff, the total loss of privacy and self-determination) meant to degrade and dehumanize clearly finds its parallel in the institution of slavery. One need only substitute patrollers and overseers for marshals and guards. Still, there is another metaphor all three writers seek to establish in making connections between the condition of being imprisoned and being enslaved. In all three narratives, prison is not only a literal reality; it is also invoked as a metaphor for African Americans' status vis-à-vis the dominant culture. The routine surveillance of Black urban communities by police (acting as occupation forces), for example, parallels surveillance inside the prison. Literature by Black men, across class backgrounds, repeatedly points to police surveillance of Black male bodies that occurs both inside and outside of prison walls. By contrast, the surveillance of women's bodies and lives that goes on outside the prison tends to be more insidious and is more rigorously bound to class. For instance, poor women who are beneficiaries of social programs can expect to endure demeaning surveillance and harassment from the intrusion of local, state, and federal agencies into even the most intimate details of their daily lives. Davis, Shakur, and Brown, like other activists of the Movement, charge that for Black people, America itself is a prison. Shakur, for instance, declares that "Any Black person in amerika, if they are honest with themselves, have [sic] got to come to the conclusion that they don't know what it feels like to be free. We aren't free politically, economically, or socially. We have very little power over what happens in our lives" (*Assata*, 60). Shakur's claims are echoed by H. Bruce Franklin.

Franklin asserts: "From the point of view of the Afro-American experience, imprisonment is first of all the loss of a *people's* freedom. The questions of individual freedom, class freedom, and even of human freedom derive from that social imprisonment. From this point of view, American society as a whole constitutes the primary prison" (Franklin, 224). The notion of America itself as a prison necessarily leads to a more expansive definition of what it means to be a "political prisoner." After explaining that a political prisoner is "someone who has been illegally incarcerated because of his or her opinions or who, having been convicted of a crime, is brutalized while in prison because of his or her opinions or who is convicted of committing a crime for political reasons," Williams writes, in *Inadmissible Evidence*, that she believes all African Americans are political prisoners because the combination of racism and economic inequity almost ensures that they receive neither fair trials nor just sentences (Williams, 83). Davis indicates in her autobiography that "at least ninety-five percent of the women in the House of D[etention] were either Black or Puerto Rican" (*Autobiography*, 61). Both Shakur and Davis attribute such high numbers to the criminalization of poverty, a phenomenon resulting in the overwhelming majority of women inmates being jailed for petty shoplifting, prostitution, running numbers, or passing bad checks (*Assata*, 54). Because of racism, White women facing similar charges are often released on their own recognizance. For poor women of color, jail is often simply a holding place before they are even charged with crimes. Like other activists, Shakur ultimately concludes that "prisons are part of this government's genocidal war against Black and Third World people" (65). Current statistics lend credence to her claim. Not only are more and more prisons being erected, but projections are that most will continue to warehouse a disproportionate number of African Americans and other people of color. Although Blacks, for example, make up only 12 percent of the U.S. population, the Bureau of Justice Statistics reports that Black men accounted for roughly 46 percent of U.S. prisoners in 1997 (Davidson, 38). Between 1985 and 1995, the number of Black men incarcerated rose 130 percent. The increase in numbers for Whites, by comparison, was 90 percent. During this same period, the number of Black women incarcerated rose nearly 200 percent (Davidson, 42). Many argue that discriminatory sentencing accounts in large part for the racial disparity. "In

1995, for instance, the National Criminal Justice Commission reported that African-Americans . . . 13 percent of all monthly drug users, represented 74 percent of those sentenced to prison for drug possession" (Davidson, 37). Black activists maintain that the proliferation of prisons (and the recent alarming trend toward profit-generating privatization) constitutes, in many ways, another form of slavery for the disproportionately African American population that penal institutions continue to house.

In self-consciously invoking parallels between their own experiences and those of the emancipation narrators, Davis, Shakur, and Brown take the historical experience of slavery and translate it metaphorically into the contemporary context in order to interrogate ways in which some conditions have remained for African Americans fundamentally the same. That is, African American communities continue to be victimized by manifestations of colonial domination and exploitation, state repression, and systemic racism, albeit in different forms. The comparison of contemporary conditions for a large population of African Americans to conditions under slavery works as a rhetorical strategy to underscore the urgency of the writers' own calls for social justice. Like the emancipation narrators, each activist uses autobiography as a form of political intervention. That is, in addition to telling their own experiences, they use their narratives as sites of critical pedagogy to share stories of the struggle and to convey other important (usually historical) information that might otherwise be lost.

Chapter 3

On Becoming
Activists' Reflections on
Their Formative Experiences

There is perhaps no literary form more conducive than autobiography to activists' efforts to emphatically link the personal to the political. In her essay, "Feminist Politicization: A Comment," bell hooks proposes that "[t]here is much exciting work to be done when we use confession and memory as a way to theorize experience, to deepen our awareness, as part of the process of radical politicization" (hooks, *Talking Back*, 110). The autobiographical form allows activists to offer as models—for understanding, imitating, and critiquing—their own processes of coming into revolutionary consciousness. Narratives like Davis's, Shakur's, and Brown's, as hooks might argue, illuminate the "conditions that enable the construction of radical black subjectivity as well as the obstacles that impede its development" (hooks, *Black Looks*, 56). How the women use their respective autobiographies to theorize and politicize their experiences, to teach and to critique, is the subject of this chapter.

All three narratives are written in teleological form. That is, each writer rereads the early years of her life in such a way as to illuminate how she arrived at her present circumstances. Teleological narratives posit a linear trajectory using what is known at the end to generate the beginning. Historically, most autobiographies have followed this form. Relatively recent autobiographical writing and the critical theory that has accompanied it, however, have effectively exposed the fiction implicit in such a project. Such writers and critics remind us that any attempt to connect, and thereby interpret the meaning of, experiences from our past implicates us in a narrative process. This narrative process involves selecting or privileging some events at the expense of others. Ultimately, how we order or make meaning of past experience is determined by our own epistemological orientation. This concept is nicely elucidated by Annie Dillard in her essay "To Fashion a Text." Dillard suggests that in simply recalling the past, one is also engaged in *creating* that past. She cautions: "If you prize your memories as they are, by all means avoid—eschew—writing a memoir. Because it is a certain way to lose them. You can't put together a memoir without cannibalizing your own life for parts. The work battens on your memories. And it replaces them" (Dillard, 70). According to Dillard, writing actually alters memory because once "you've written, you can no longer remember anything but the writing" (71). That is, where there were previously only a series of impressions, the act of writing imposes closure by fixing meaning. Similarly, Frank Kermode has argued for the way in which remembering is inextricably tied up with forgetting. Memory invents the past because we remember some things only at the expense of forgetting others.

In autobiographical practice, subjects manipulate the fiction of narrative to make sense of the past through the awareness of the present (a condition Kermode calls the "double consciousness" of autobiographical writing). In *Rewriting the Self: History, Memory, Narrative*, Mark Freeman refers to the trope of "development" (which has long been an integral aspect of autobiographical writing) as a kind of fiction. The idea of "development" refers to a subject's apparent move from a naive or less sophisticated state of (self/social/political) awareness to a point of greater self-consciousness, understanding, and/or agency. Classic African American autobiographical texts in this tradition include Frederick Douglass's *Narrative of the Life* (1845), and the *Autobiography of Malcolm X* (1964) with Alex Haley. Freeman indicates that attempting to explain present conditions by artificially constructing a continuum (typically composed of cause-and-effect relationships) leading from the past to the present inevitably results in a substantial delimiting of the field of signification of past experiences. Thus, events that may have had any number of meanings at the time are reduced to a single meaning that enables them to fit more convincingly into a narrative of development. Freeman perceptively notes that "the most fundamental trick one is perpetrating in the very act of telling is the idea of starting at the beginning, when in reality 'you have started at the end' " (Freeman, 95).

The fiction of development, however, is an important and perhaps indispensable aspect of *political autobiography*. It is, in a sense, a *necessary* fiction in which Brown, Davis, and Shakur (along with other writers of political autobiography) all participate in realizing the conventions and objectives of the genre. Invoking a model of development, activists are able to demonstrate the move toward revolutionary consciousness as foremost a *process*. That is, revolutionaries are not so much born as *made* (i.e., by the circumstances of their social milieu and by their exposure to critical pedagogy). Depicting this as process has a deliberately demystifying effect that both humanizes the subjects and allows for the possibility that their examples might be readily repeated. Shakur's and Brown's narratives do a particularly nice job of illustrating the birth and development of revolutionary consciousness through the writers' retelling of significant, early personal experiences that both reshaped their understanding of the dynamics of race, class, and gender oppression in America and motivated their eventual involvement in political struggle. Such key moments become framing devices for the narrative reconstruction of their pasts. Brown's comment about her own narrative strategy explains one of her objectives in writing A Taste: "When I talked about growing up, all of us have gone through that process. I didn't spring forth saying 'Power to the People!' It was a gradual process" (Sinclair, "A Conversation," 24). The attention they give to theorizing the significance of such moments in retrospect is an important characteristic of political autobiography, since representing how one's political consciousness is awakened serves to demystify the process by which revolutionaries are created. As Shakur maintains: "Black revolutionaries do not drop from the moon. We are created by our conditions. Shaped by our oppression. We are being manufactured in droves in the ghetto streets, places like attica, san quentin, bedford hills, leavenworth, and sing sing" (Assata, 52). Importantly, the writers are also able to illustrate that their experiences are not that different (in terms of the culture's treatment of and expectations for them) from those of thousands of other Black women in America. Their sharing of their early experiences is a kind of testifying in which they express solidarity with other women. As bell hooks maintains, "Critical pedagogy, the sharing of information and knowledge by black women with black women, is crucial for the development of radical black female subjectivity (not because black women can only learn from one another, but because the circumstances of racism, sexism, and class exploitation ensure that other groups will not necessarily seek to further [black women's] self-determination)" (hooks, *Black Looks*, 56). Both Shakur and Brown seem to recognize this imperative to share such information. Brown even maintains that she wrote *A Taste* intending other Black women as her primary audience.

In their respective autobiographies, Davis, Brown, and Shakur all theorize and politicize their past personal experiences, covering several important subjects and highlighting, in the process, ways in which the personal is political. Although each mentions the zeitgeist of the unfolding Civil Rights Movement as perhaps the most immediate factor underlying her growing spirit of restlessness and determination to enter organized political struggle, all three women also acknowledge the significance of much earlier formative experiences in shaping their political consciousness. In the recounting of their childhood and young adult years, they endeavor to address the significance of race, class, and gender oppression in Black women's socialization as well as its impact on the African American community in general.

The perils of growing up Black and female in a racist and misogynist society are poignantly illustrated by both Brown and Shakur. Each writes about her own vulnerability to sexual abuse and exploitation by men, White and Black. Referring to the constant harassment she endured from customers as well as her employer while working as a waitress in Greenwich Village, Shakur remarks: "Any Black woman, practically anywhere in America, can tell you about being approached, propositioned and harassed by white men. Many consider all Black women prostitutes" (*Assata*, 106). As both Brown's and Shakur's experiences attest, however, there is little relief from the prospect of such dehumanizing treatment even within their own communities. Both writers recount harrowing episodes of being nearly gang-raped by male agemates whom they had dared to trust. After being set up by a young man who invites her to accompany him to an alleged party underway in a nearby housing project, Shakur discovers upon their arrival that she is to be the only female present. When the other boys quickly corner her, she manages to preempt the rape by threatening to demolish the apartment. The boys leave the scene only after repeated pleas from the boy in whose home they are gathered. His fear of his mother's reprisal, upon coming home to find their apartment in shambles, is enough to make him call off their intended assault. With the assistance of a neighbor, Shakur is escorted out of the apartment and into the safety of a cab. What is most interesting about the episode (aside from Shakur's ingenuity and quick thinking) is that it is the threat of property damage (as opposed to any respect or consideration for her as a human being) that saves Shakur from being raped. Up until the time she hurls the first piece of furniture, she is invisible to them. In the aftermath of the episode, Shakur recalls that she was more shaken than anything else by the boys' apparent hatred for her, since it was intense and yet profoundly *impersonal*. For them, gang rape was not personal; any girl would do and any girl anywhere was thus equally vulnerable.

In *A Taste* Brown relates a similar sexual assault. Like Shakur, she was only thirteen when she was nearly raped while attending a friend's party. Her response at the time reveals the extent to which sexual assault on girls was a common occurrence. As her assailants struggled to pin her down, Brown recalls her own sense of powerlessness and subsequent resignation to what all of her experiences to date had taught her to eventually expect. She writes: "For some reason, I could not scream. I thought about how unbelievable it was that I would have to 'give it up' in this way, for it was accomplished as far as I was concerned. I silently put up a futile resistance and hoped only that it would not hurt and I would not bleed like a dog" (*A Taste*, 43). Notably, Brown's language here (specifically, the notion of being forced to "give it up") foreshadows the coercive rhetoric she later encounters from some of the men in the Black Panther Party. Before Brown is actually raped, the assault is unexpectedly called off by the leader of the gang, who reminds the others that Brown is, after all, an "Avenue bitch" (i.e., a girl from their own territory) and on those grounds, "pulling a train" (i.e., gang rape) would be morally wrong. As with Shakur, the boys stop not out of any concern for Brown's welfare, but because they realize that they would be violating their own property.

Brown's and Shakur's experiences point to similar misogynist objectification of women that finds its source in the larger patriarchal structure of American society. Like Shakur, who maintains that "it was a common thing back then for boys to downgrade girls and cuss at them in the street," Brown remembers similar harassment. The endeavor to simply mind one's own business could be met with anything from verbal abuse to physical violence. Brown recalls at sixteen, for instance, being kicked in the face and then trampled on the street by a boy who became irate after she politely declined his sexual advances (*A Taste*, 61). Brown notes further the way she and other young girls growing up in the housing projects of Philadelphia were regarded as property of warring gangs, and therefore could not socialize with boys living in territories outside their own. Although girls were not above risk in their own territories as well, girls who violated this code of the streets could expect to be violently attacked and/or raped. These territorial battles between men, often fought over the bodies of women, imitate on a much smaller scale the way nationalist struggles tend to be waged in the global arena. Brown's recollections thus symbolically illustrate one way nationalist expression can be potentially repressive for women.

The analysis Shakur offers of the impact of misogyny on male-female relations is insightful for the way it contextualizes Black women's responses to Black men (*Assata*, 116). Shakur challenges the oft-repeated criticism of Black women as excessively materialistic in their demands on Black men, by recasting such overt materialism in the context of misogynist treatment and devaluation by Black men. Shakur recalls her own experience growing up: "It was common for [boys] to go to bed with girls and talk about them like dogs the next day. It was common for boys to deny they were fathers of their babies. And it was common for boys to beat girls up and knock them around" (116). Black women's alleged materialism (often expressed as disdain for Black men unable to provide financially), then, is a mirroring of the same emotional disengagement acted out by their male counterparts. Shakur's perspective is powerful since it is one that rarely surfaces in contemporary popular (as opposed to scholarly) debates about the quality of Black male-female relationships. Because the reality of misogyny as a problem within America as a whole rarely enters such discussions, Black women, in simply acting out of self-preservation, are frequently reduced to the stereotype of "castrating bitches."

Shakur takes her analysis a step further to propose the quality of Black men's and women's responses to each other as a carryover from the dynamics of life on the slave plantation. Unable to turn their rage and frustration on the appropriate target (i.e., the master/oppressor), Black people, Shakur writes, learned to turn it on each other. As scholarship by bell hooks, Angela Davis, and Jacqueline Jones attests, Black women on the slave plantation were subject to the sexual denigration of both White men and Black men.[1] If Black women can be said to have internalized negative attitudes toward Black men as but one byproduct of slavery, then as Shakur argues, the same must also hold true for Black men's internalization of White men's attitudes toward Black women. It is significant that Shakur and Brown address these early experiences with misogyny because the reality of how women and men are socialized provides important insight into why the otherwise progressive political movements that emerged out of the late 1960s were often compromised by regressive gender/sexual politics.

Brown also writes extensively about the significance of class in shaping her early experiences. Reared by her mother and abandoned by her father, Brown's class consciousness is shaped both by the nature of her experiences growing up in the urban environment of North Philadelphia and by the stories she remembers hearing repeated about her mother's own life of sacrifice and hardship. Horace Scott's implicit rejection of his daughter is a source of pain Brown recounts among her earliest memories. Scott, who had an affair with Dorothy Clark that resulted in Brown's conception, never publicly acknowledged his daughter. Furthermore, his abandonment of Brown and her mother left them in financial hardship. Because Scott enjoyed some degree of affluence as a physician, Brown always felt as if she were cheated out of her birthright. The language Brown uses to describe York Street, where she spent her earliest years, vividly renders the violence of poverty. Reminiscent of the imagery in Ann Petry's 1946 novel *The Street* (set in Harlem), Brown writes of her own York Street: "Its darkness and its smells of industrial dirt and poverty permeated and overwhelmed everything. There were always piles of trash and garbage in the street that never moved except by force of wind, and then only from one side of the street to the other. Overhead utility wires in disrepair ribboned the skyline. Cavernous sewage drains on the street corners spit forth their stench. Soot languished on the concrete walkways, on the steps and sides of the houses, and even in the air" (*A Taste*, 18). As horrible as York Street is, however, this is not apparent to Brown until she has some basis for comparison. Only after

---

[1] See bell hooks, *Ain't I a Woman*, Angela Davis, *Women, Race & Class*, and Jacqueline Jones, *Labor of Love, Labor of Sorrow*.

attending a Halloween party at the comparatively lavish home of her second-grade school mate, Barbara Keesal, a little Jewish girl (26) is Brown abruptly awakened to the clash between America's haves and have-nots. Although Brown's mother endeavors to shield her as much as possible from the violence of poverty, her bourgeois aspirations for her daughter only work to highlight the disparity between their own condition and that of the privileged White and middle-class "colored" families with whom Brown is encouraged to associate. Brown remembers that after visiting the immaculate homes of some of her White classmates, the return to the dismal squalor of her own home was often unbearable. She recounts a sense of alienation and diminishing self-worth in having to circulate between these two vastly different worlds.

The time Brown spends with her mother's sister Francine (a college graduate), and her husband, the minister, in Pasadena, California, offers Brown another opportunity to observe blatant disparities between her economic circumstances and those of others. Brown mentions Francine as a way of critiquing class elitism. Noting that Francine was the only member of her mother's family to have gone to college, Brown situates Francine's success in the context of others' struggles. According to Brown, Francine's older sisters (who included Dorothy Clark) "had paved her way with their hard-earned wages" (A Taste, 72). Brown thus recalls with bitter irony Francine's snubbing of her years later when she arrives in California in need of a place to stay.

All three women reveal that the need to assimilate European cultural practices was something taught by the dominant culture and reinforced within African American families as one consequence of oppression and colonization. Like Brown's mother, Shakur's family seeks to provide her with the values and trappings necessary for assimilation into middle-class, bourgeois culture. Both women recall the constant discourse around the need to be as good as White people (or in other words, to be found acceptable by their standards), noting also the self-alienation that arises from such a project. In her effort to satisfy standards defined by others, Shakur writes that "in many ways [she] was living a double existence" (Assata, 37). This sentiment is echoed in Davis's narrative as well. Relaying the way in which she struggled against the dominant culture's negative expectations for and assumptions about Black people, Davis proclaims: "I had made up my mind that I was going to prove to the world that I was just as good, just as intelligent, just as capable of achieving as any white person" (*Autobiography*, 93).

Similar to Brown's mother, who encouraged her daughter's association with other children outside their own economic and social class, Shakur's grandparents desired that she pursue friendships with the children of other so-called "respectable" families, rather than the "alley rats" whose company Shakur most enjoyed. Shakur makes apparent the irony in her grandparents' class bias when she reveals that, unbeknownst to them, one of her grandmother's "favorite little decent kids' favorite game was playing show and tell with his ding-a-ling and threatening to pee on everybody" (*Assata*, 22). Shakur notes that her grandparents' class values and assumptions remained a point of contention between her and them throughout her childhood years. The self-determination she exhibits before her grandparents is later evident in her activist work and undergirds her expressions of solidarity with a broad range of people. Shakur's resistance to her grandparents' ideas about how she ought to conduct her friendships also offers insight into why she ultimately rejects the authoritarian paramilitary ethos and structure of the Black Panther Party as antithetical to her own mode of being.

Despite the elitist values transmitted by her family, however, Shakur notes that her grandparents instilled in her a strong sense of self-worth and racial pride. Most importantly, Shakur recalls that her family forbade her to behave in a subservient manner around Whites (19). Rather, she was constantly encouraged to speak up, especially in their presence. Shakur indicates that her family also valued reading and that her grandfather often traveled to the colored library to check out books for her to read (23). Just as she credits her grandfather with nurturing her interest in and love for books, Shakur credits her aunt, Evelyn, with expanding her cultural horizons by exposing her to museums and galleries, films, restaurants, and plays. While living with Evelyn in New York City, Shakur also witnessed, for the first time, the proximity of wealth to poverty. Through her friendship with Li'l Bit, a classmate, she discovers the reality of squalor, despair, and hopelessness for those trapped in abject poverty (134).

Davis writes that her first awareness of class difference came with her enrollment in elementary school. Prior to that time, she had, like most children, just assumed everyone lived like her own family. In interacting with other children at the segregated Carrie A. Tuggle school in Birmingham, however, she came to recognize her family as among the "not so poor." Though far from wealthy, both of her parents were employed and had the benefit of college educations; their two incomes were enough to ensure that she and her siblings had three meals a day, a home of their own, and an ample supply of clothing. Like Brown, Davis exposes the Protestant work ethic as a myth; that is, while Black people often worked hard, their labor and diligence rarely resulted in prosperity. While Brown has stated that her mother never knew relief from suffering, Davis suggests that her parents might just as easily have shared the same plight as so many other hardworking families had they not been fortunate enough to receive certain breaks (*Autobiography*, 90). Davis indicates that she first became conscious of her own privilege relative to some of the other children when she observed that some of her friends were too poor to afford lunch each day and so stood outside looking in while she and the other children ate. Davis recalls that she was so disturbed by this state of affairs that she began pilfering coins from a bag her father kept stashed in the kitchen cupboard. Each day, she would bring the money to school to distribute to the children so that they too would be able to eat.

Like Shakur, Davis evinces early on a sense of solidarity with those less fortunate than she. Over the duration of their activism, both she and Shakur ultimately surrender class privilege in aligning themselves with the economically dispossessed. The fact that Davis is both born into a solid middle-class family and formally educated at some of the world's most prestigious institutions, furthermore, places her in the historical tradition of Denmark Vesey and other middle-class radicals, who in forfeiting their birthright, essentially commit class suicide. One noteworthy aspect of all three narratives is that they illustrate the extent to which movement across class lines was not uncommon during the era. All document, for example, the easy intermingling of students and nonstudents on college campuses and within the surrounding communities during the late 1960s and early 1970s.

Shakur writes that her grandparents owned and operated a restaurant/resort along Carolina Beach that became a haven for vacationing Black families prohibited, by segregation, from most other public and private beaches. Although Shakur's early memories of time spent on her grandparents' beachfront property in Wilmington, North Carolina, sharply contrast with the impoverished, urban landscape defining Brown's earliest memories, there are points at which their experiences overlap considerably. While an adolescent living with her mother in New York, Shakur's rebellion against her family leads to her immersion in the urban underclass of New York City, where she (as Brown did after moving to California) encounters a host of colorful characters. Some of her renegade associations during this period include: Tina and her mother—the "five-finger discount" woman (*Assata*, 77), the paranoid schizophrenic she meets in Greenwich Village (101), and the transvestite, "Miss Shirley," who expresses motherly concern for her welfare. Both Brown (at age twenty-two) and Shakur (illegally, at thirteen) work as cocktail waitresses—Shakur at a dive called Tony's in the City (109), and Brown at the more upscale Pink Pussycat strip club in West Hollywood (75). Clearly, both Brown and Shakur gain an education of sorts from life on the streets, learning in different ways to fend for themselves.

While all three writers retell their memories of de facto segregation and of bumping up against the White world for the first time, Davis and Shakur, who both spent part of their young lives in the American South, also address de jure racial segregation and its impact on their awakening political consciousness. Aside from their experiences in school, Shakur and Davis each highlight a childhood memory that exemplifies the often creative and ingenious ways Black people living in the South resisted racist treatment and dehumanization. Shakur, for instance, remembers longing as a child to be able to play in an amusement park in Wilmington designated for Whites only. Unable to forestall her daughter's pleading any longer, Shakur's mother eventually concocts a plan to get Shakur and her sister into the park. By speaking Spanish and pretending to comprehend very little English, she leads the park attendants to believe that she and her two daughters are foreign nationals visiting the United States. Anxious not to appear bigoted before foreigners, the park attendants apologize for the apparent misunderstanding and politely usher them into the park.

Davis recalls a similar incident in which she and her sister, Fania, wandered into a shoe store in Birmingham with the intent of trying on shoes in the front of the store, the location normally reserved for Whites. When they are approached by a clerk (both annoyed and surprised by their apparent disregard for propriety), she and Fania begin conversing in French, with Fania pretending to understand slightly less English than Davis. As with Shakur's experience, the proprietors of the shop are chagrined over having mistaken them for "ordinary Negroes" and go out of their way to atone for the apparent error. Angela and Fania, however, up the ante by revealing their true identity just before leaving. Their gesture both underscores the Whites' gullibility and insecurity, and forces them to confront the ugliness and absurdity of their own racial bigotry. The fact that Davis and Shakur include these incidents in their narratives suggests that each saw the experience as a pivotal moment in her developing consciousness. Certainly, such early confrontations with the White world made palpable the gross disparity between the kinds of opportunities available to Whites and those open to Blacks.

Notwithstanding the clashes between Black and White worlds they experienced during their early years, Davis, Shakur, and Brown devote considerably more attention to their memories of particular dynamics *within the Black communities* in which they lived. All three women, for instance, address the devastating impact of learned self-hatred on their own self-image and on their interaction with others in their communities, critiquing in particular the impact of negative values surrounding hair texture and length, skin tone, and physical features. In her narrative, Shakur recalls the sometimes vicious signifying that went on among her agemates on the playground: "We would call each other 'jungle bunnies' and 'bush boogies.' We would talk about each other's ugly, big lips and flat noses. We would call each other pickaninnies and nappy-haired so-and-so's. . . . Black made any insult worse. When you called somebody a 'bastard,' that was bad. But when you called somebody a 'Black bastard,' now that was terrible. In fact, when i was growing up, being called 'Black,' period, was grounds for fighting" (*Assata*, 30). The aforesaid passage is followed by Shakur's detailed elaboration of the means by which she and other Black girls learned early to reject their full lips, kinky hair, and broad noses as undesirable features. Indoctrinated thus into self-hatred, those victimized by society almost inevitably went on to victimize others. This is illustrated in Shakur's recollections of her interaction with a young admirer and classmate named Joe. Like Brown, who remembers her fear of associating with Francine, a classmate ostracized for being black (i.e., dark-skinned) and poor (*A Taste*, 64), Shakur recalls the racist way she once treated Joe. Shakur writes that when Joe finally summoned the courage to ask her to be his girl, she turned him down on the grounds that he was "too black and ugly" to be considered desirable by any of her peers (*Assata*, 72). Shakur writes that she was haunted thereafter by the hurt and hatred her rejection had inflicted. The incident becomes a critical point in the development of her political consciousness. She writes: "After that i never said 'Black' and 'ugly' in the same sentence and never thought it. Of course, i couldn't undo all the years of self-hatred and brainwashing in that short time, but it was a beginning" (72).

While Davis decided early on that she "would never . . . harbor or express the desire to be white" (*Autobiography*, 85), much of the early part of Brown's narrative chronicles her struggle with self-hatred and her longing to escape the limitations of Black identity in a racist society. Brown recalls that her longing for acceptance by Whites rendered her "a formidable little wretch." She confesses: "I did anything to belong among them, those white children and white teachers" (*A Taste*, 30). Brown's critical tone in retrospect signifies her change in critical/racial consciousness. She notes that her efforts to assimilate growing up meant that she readily imitated everything associated with being White and also settled for the dubious honor of being a token among her White classmates, first at Thaddeus Stevens (31) and then at Girls High. Additionally, Brown recalls shunning girls who were "too dark" or had hair that was "too nappy," or who manifested features considered "too Negroid" based on Euroamerican standards of beauty. Her early self-concept is reinforced not only by messages from the dominant culture but also by messages she receives from her mother, who is likewise victimized by her socialization in American culture. Brown remembers being constantly reminded by her mother of the ways in which she was physically different from (read: better than) the other Black children in their neighborhood (21). Cooed over for her comparatively light skin, Caucasoid features, and "good" hair, Brown recalls her mother's constant doting on her as a child. Tapping into African American collective consciousness, she recites a verse frequently heard in Black communities: "If you white, you right. / If you yellow, you mellow. / If you brown, stick around. / If you black, git [sic] back. / Way back!" (31). A variation of this rhyme also appears in Shakur's text (*Assata*, 271). The saying, which

parodies the voice of the oppressor, reflects both the community's inter-
nalizing of the dominant culture's way of thinking *and* the community's
analysis of how racism circumscribes their lives. Davis implies that she,
too, having both light skin and wavy as opposed to kinky hair, was victimized by her community's acceptance of this sentiment. She recalls
that she often lamented the fact that she was born with light skin and
"good" hair, since this was a point of contention for many of her agemates (*Autobiography*, 96). Describing the hurt of being ostracized by her
own people solely because of her appearance, Davis recalls feeling less
wounded by the epithets "black" or "nigger" (i.e., from other African
Americans) than by hearing someone say, "Just because you're bright
and got good hair, you think you can act like you're white" (96). She
goes on to acknowledge that "it was a typical charge laid against light-
skinned children." Elaine Brown suggests that when the black aesthetic
shifted in the 1960s, Davis was again victimized by reactionary senti-
ments among Black radicals. Although the analysis is probably reductive, Brown charges that Davis was "driven away [from the BPP and into
the ranks of the CPUSA] by the stupidity of niggers. They attacked her
because she was too light-skinned and too well educated, which they
translated as too bourgeois" (*A Taste*, 291).

Brown describes increasing racial and class alienation beginning with
her junior high school years. Set apart (by two moves) from her childhood friends on York Street, by racism from her White classmates, and
by the elitism of her middle-class Black classmates, she writes: "I was
beginning to accept a life outside of life. Once my mother and I moved
to Tioga, I became committed to living almost exclusively in my own
world" (45). This status as outsider is a recurring theme in Brown's text;
although her sense of alienation is alleviated at times, it ultimately never
finds resolution. Like Shakur, Brown becomes something of a renegade
during her teen years. Her romantic relationship at sixteen with Bob
Ludwig, a White Jewish boy one year her senior, constitutes a critical
moment in her awakening racial consciousness. Initially unable to understand the necessity of keeping their relationship a secret from Ludwig's family, Brown soon gets an education in the politics of race in
America (58). Ludwig's family's rejection of her explodes her original
assumption that simply emulating White ways of being and knowing
would secure her unconditional entrance and acceptance into their

communities. The specter of race stuns Brown back into an awareness of her outsider status, socially alienated from both Black and White circles. The sense of aloneness and alienation Brown endures during her early years is eventually carried over into her association with the Party. It is also one of the reasons she finds in Huey Newton a soulmate. According to Brown, they found common ground based on their shared status as outsiders.

The gradual change in Brown's racial and class consciousness is signified by her chapter titles. Chapter 4, which depicts the early part of her affair with her wealthy White lover, Jay Kennedy (as the *culmination* of her alienation from Black working-class identity), is titled "Some Other Life," while chapter 6, which inaugurates her association with the Party, is aptly titled "Getting Black." Brown's friendship with Beverlee, described in chapter 5, is the bridge between the two. Through Beverlee, Brown reestablishes contact with her origins. In 1969, two years after her arrival in California, Brown agrees, as a favor to Beverlee, to offer piano lessons to a group of young Black girls living in the Jordan Housing Project in Watts. The commitment forces Brown to confront again, after escaping temporarily into the oblivion and opulence of Jay Kennedy's world, the reality of her own origins. Taken aback by the similarities between herself and her prospective music students, she concedes: "They were *me*. It was me I saw. There was my face, my pain, my nothing-little-nigger-girl expression lingering on their faces and in their eyes" (100). Brown recognizes in them the same internalized sense of worthlessness by which she herself was victimized. The language Brown uses to recreate the encounter illustrates her own change in critical consciousness, as she implicitly challenges the dichotomy between "them" and "us." Seeing herself reflected in the young girls, she writes: "I saw the poverty of our lives, the poverty of little black girls who live on the same planet, in the same world where people, people like me, drank expensive bottles of champagne that clouded the mind with bubbles that obliterated them, us; where men, powerful men, made big decisions about their own lives and footnotes about the lives of them, us, that pushed us back, back into nothing little corners on the outskirts of life" (101). Brown's replacement of "them" with "us" captures her move from a position of distance to one of solidarity with other Black women, based on a shared experience of race, class, and gender oppression. The passage is also obviously self-critical; Brown's inclusion of herself among those who long to forget (by attempting to escape their past and their origins) suggests a sense of her own complicity with the structures responsible for maintaining the status quo. Her life with Kennedy is exposed as an illusion, a longing to escape. Any remaining ambivalence over the distinction between "us" and "them" is resolved for her following a confrontation with Kennedy in which she finally recognizes that there can be no real future to their relationship. Realizing that he will never leave his family to be with her, the possibility of escape into Kennedy's world (where wealth and influence shield her from the sting of racism) is no longer a viable option. When the prospect for escape dissolves, she must finally acknowledge that there is more commonalty than difference between her own status and that of the girls in the housing project (since as Black women, they share victimization by the same social, economic, and political forces). Brown thus refigures herself into the "them" which she then renames as the collective "us." Even though her initial desire is to flee from any responsibility to her prospective students, Brown ultimately is unable to turn her back on the girls because she recognizes herself in them.

Brown's, Davis's, and Shakur's discussion of their early years includes considerable attention to their formal educational experiences in the public school system. All three women challenge the Eurocentric bias in American education (their critiques are still largely applicable today) while advocating the importance of self-education to combat miseducation. Like other political activists, all recognize education as an emphatically political arena where relations of power are inseparable from the way knowledge is defined and disseminated. Clearly, this awareness leads George Jackson, for example, to warn that "the most damaging thing a people in a colonial situation can do is to allow their children to attend any educational facility organized by the dominant enemy culture" (Jackson, *Soledad*, 12). In the process of rewriting history and theorizing their own experiences, the women's texts create a critical pedagogy with important social applications beyond their texts. Criticism of American formal (mis)education is an important component of all three texts, particularly pertaining to the systematic exclusion of the African American presence in the shaping of American history and culture. The term "miseducation," which invokes Carter G. Woodson's *The Mis-education of the Negro*, describes the way information is deliberately and systematically controlled (distorted, withheld, or otherwise manipulated) to ensure the continuation of an oppressive order. Such an order secures the privileges of a small minority—from which even most members of the dominant culture are excluded—over the interests of the vast majority.

Shakur's narrative includes a critique of educational structure as well as content. Maintaining, for instance, that the compartmentalization of knowledge, at all levels of the American educational system, actually undermines critical literacy, she explains: "For the most part, we receive fragments of unrelated knowledge, and our education follows no logical format or pattern. It is exactly this kind of education that produces people who don't have the ability to think for themselves and who are easily manipulated" (*Assata*, 35). The often rigid separation of disciplines and the increasing trend toward specialization in American institutions of higher learning means that it is increasingly difficult to make meaningful analyses of experiences that require an understanding of the way ideas and events are interconnected. Shakur's text thus advocates a more holistic, and by implication counterdisciplinary, approach to teaching and learning. Like Davis and Brown, though, she is also critical at the level of content, pointing out the overwhelmingly Eurocentric focus of American education. "When i think of how racist, how Eurocentric our so-called education in amerika is," she writes, "it staggers my mind" (136). Because in most states education is required by law until children are at least sixteen years of age, the forced imposition of a Eurocentric curriculum on a multicultural populace amounts to little more than cultural imperialism. To this end, Shakur recasts nonmajority students' inability to thrive in such climates as a form of resistance rather than an indication of failure. Retrospectively, she writes: "when i think back to some of those kids who were labeled 'troublemakers' and 'problem students,' i realize that many of them were unsung heroes who fought to maintain some sense of dignity and self-worth" (136). Shakur describes, for example, her junior high school classmates' animosity toward a music instructor who, in presuming the inherent superiority of European classical forms, effectively alienated an entire class of predominantly Black and Puerto Rican students. The students' dislike for the instructor, Shakur suggests, was less a result of their inability to relate to classical music (appreciation of difference is learned through exposure and understand-

ing) than of the teacher's blatant condescension toward them, and her
implicit rejection of musical forms outside her own cultural frame of
reference. Shakur recalls: "We hated her because she thought the music
she liked was so superior. She didn't recognize that we had our own
music and that we loved music" (136). Because the teacher was incapa-
ble of reciprocally extending the cultural respect she demanded of the
students, she was unsuccessful in gaining their cooperation during her
class. As Iris Marion Young notes, one of the major aspects of the oppression of cultural imperialism is "the group-connected experience of being
regarded by others with aversion." Consistent with Shakur's portrait of
the music instructor, Young argues that "much of the oppressive experience of cultural imperialism occurs in mundane contexts of interaction—in the gestures, speech, tone of voice, movement, and reactions of
others" (Young, 123). Of course, the irony is that the teacher's own
prejudices prevent her from recognizing and utilizing the common bond
she does share with her students: their mutual love of music.

As she grows older, Shakur is shocked to discover just how little she
was ever taught about her own history. She discovers only belatedly,
through her association with the Golden Drums (a politically conscious
Black campus organization at Manhattan Community College), that
there exists a long history of African American resistance corresponding
in duration to the history of racist oppression. She writes: "I had grown
up believing the slaves hadn't fought back. I remember feeling ashamed
when they talked about slavery in school. The teachers made it seem
that Black people had nothing to do with the official 'emancipation'
from slavery. White people had freed us" (*Assata*, 175). Out of her association with the Golden Drums, she becomes an avid reader. She goes
on to describe the process of self-education by which she began to both
unlearn and compensate for holes left by her formal education. Because
she goes into considerable detail recounting and rewriting the distorted
history she was taught about the Civil War and the abolition of slavery
(175–80), for example, she also offers the revised information for her
readers' consideration. That is, she shifts from talking about her own
changing consciousness to focusing on her readers' education. In her
role as teacher, she reminds her readers that the Civil War was not a
humanitarian effort to free the slaves, but a struggle between the compet-
ing economic interests of "rich, white Southern slave owners and rich,

white Northern industrialists" (178). Shakur additionally quotes from the *History of the Negro Race in America, Vol. II* to expose the oft-perpetuated half-truth of Abraham Lincoln as the "Great Emancipator" (177). She cites excerpts both from Lincoln's letters (176) and from the Lincoln-Douglas debates (178) that attest to Lincoln's moral indifference to the institution of slavery and also to his convictions of Black African inferiority. Shakur's inclusion of the quotes is important because she is able to illustrate how certain information is conveniently and deliberately left out of mainstream history texts, especially those used by primary and secondary school students. Such information becomes available only to those aware and diligent enough to seek it elsewhere. For those either illiterate or without access to library resources, the chance of encountering such information is remote.

Shakur's recollection of a trip to Alcatraz to participate in an American Indian demonstration affords an opportunity to recuperate information that has been systematically suppressed about the history of the United States' relations with other colonial subjects. A group calling itself "IAT" (Indians of All Tribes—led by Richard Oaks and American Indian Movement [AIM] activist John Trudell) occupied Alcatraz Island in San Francisco Bay in November 1969. Among their demands were that title to the territory be ceded to IAT in accordance with the provisions of an 1882 act and Title 25, U.S. Code 194 (Churchill and Vander Wall, *Agents*, 119). Shakur's solidarity with the American Indian activists at Alcatraz enables her to step outside the African American struggle to recognize critical parallels. She realizes the need to be just as critical of what she has been taught about other groups by the dominant culture's institutions as she has been about information concerning African Americans. She concludes: "As i listened to those sisters and brothers at Alcatraz i realized that the true history of any oppressed people is impossible to find in history books" (*Assata*, 199). Part of the objective of her narrative is thus to promote critical literacy, both by reeducating and by inciting the moral and intellectual discomfort of her readers. Of course, having critical literacy (and therefore the capacity to make informed choices) implies responsibility to act on what one knows. As Shakur argues: "If you are deaf, dumb, and blind to what's happening in the world, you're under no obligation to do anything. But if you know what's happening and you don't do anything but sit on your ass, then you're nothing but a punk" (207).

Although Davis's account of her early formal educational experience differs from Shakur's in that her exposure to African American history was much more extensive, her experience is marked by another kind of repression. Still, coming through the segregated school system of Birmingham afforded her advantages that an integrated setting would never have allowed. Davis notes that students were taught about their history in a nurturing environment that encouraged "strong positive identification with our people and our history" (*Autobiography*, 90). Shocked to find during a summer trip to New York that Black children there had never heard of many of the famous Black figures she was taught about in school, Davis determines: "Without a doubt, the children who attended the de jure segregated schools of the South had an advantage over those who attended the de facto segregated schools of the North. . . . At Carrie A. Tuggle Elementary School, Black identity was thrust upon us by the circumstances of oppression" (91). Shakur's experience at Gregory Elementary School (where she attended part of first and all of second grade) in the segregated school system of Wilmington, North Carolina, corroborates Davis's claim. While acknowledging the wretched material shortcomings Black children endured under segregation (i.e., inferior facilities, used and/or outdated textbooks, and scant funding, among other things), she remembers that because their teachers were, more often than not, a part of the community, Black children in segregated schools "encountered support and understanding and encouragement instead of the hostile indifference they often met in the 'integrated' schools" (*Assata*, 29). Shakur's later experiences in the integrated (but predominantly White) setting of P.S. 154 in Queens, New York, give her a solid basis for comparison. In contrast to the affirmation she received from her Black teachers in Wilmington, at P.S. 154 she encountered a string of condescending White teachers who, she says, patronized her with "little nigga grins" (32).

Despite the strong sense of Black identity she gained from her matriculation through Birmingham's segregated schools, Davis notes that her education was not without serious problems. One of these was the insidious promotion of meritocracy (the belief that people are rewarded in proportion to what they deserve/have earned), and the other was the indoctrination into defeatism, which Davis terms the "Booker T. Washington syndrome" (*Autobiography*, 92). The possibility of meaningful change, Davis remarks, was never acknowledged or addressed. She writes: "Our teachers warned us that we would have to steel ourselves for hard labor and more hard labor, sacrifices and more sacrifices. . . . It often struck me they were speaking of these obstacles as if they would always be there, part of the natural order of things, rather than the product of a system of racism, which we could eventually overturn" (92). Unlike Shakur's and Brown's experience, however, Davis's formal education does eventually encompass exposure to critical literacy. After all, Davis's education includes her transfer, on a scholarship, from the Birmingham public school system to the private, predominantly White and politically socialist Elizabeth Irwin High School in Greenwich Village, New York. There she is exposed to socialist/communist ideology as part of the curriculum. At one point in her narrative, Davis quotes from her own reading of the *Communist Manifesto*. In the process, her reader is exposed to some of the work's major tenets and social/economic implications. Similar to Shakur's endeavors to teach about American history, Davis repeatedly uses her autobiography to educate readers about communist ideology and practice. bell hooks is insightful, however, in pointing out, as a potential shortcoming of Davis's narrative, her reluctance to speak more directly to the uniqueness of her formal education. hooks argues cogently that Davis's modest minimizing of her unique background is unfortunate, since focusing on this aspect of her socialization might have been an effective way of further emphasizing the importance of education and of critical literacy in the development of radical subjectivity (hooks, *Black Looks*, 55).

The means by which Shakur and Brown first acquire critical literacy are quite different from the way Davis does. Jay Kennedy is the individual who introduces Brown to critical literacy. Perusing the volumes in his personal library, Brown becomes acquainted with, among others, the writings of Spinoza, Sartre, Hesse, and Baldwin (*A Taste*, 86). Ironically, it is Kennedy, a fifty-five-year-old White man, who is pivotal in teaching her about her own history and in making her conscious for the first time of the momentous political events unfolding around her. Brown admits that prior to meeting Kennedy, a wealthy patron of the Pink Pussycat nightclub in Hollywood where she was working in 1965, she "had not so much as batted one of [her] new false eyelashes over the recent fire that had been the Watts riots" (76). Still steeped in the learned self-hatred of her childhood years, Brown remembers being virtually oblivious to the cresting Civil Rights Movement and burgeoning Black Power struggle going on around her. Recapitulating her state of mind at the time, she writes: "I did not mind listening to him discuss the merits of the Civil Rights Movement or the Black Power Movement, and the like. Issues concerning black people, however, were not personally relevant to me" (93). In the end, she credits Kennedy with teaching her "to begin to appreciate [her]self as a black woman" (93). She recalls her earliest conversations with Kennedy as opening her eyes for the first time to the meaning of political struggle. The exchange with Kennedy, during which Brown is gently prompted to challenge her own assumptions about the meaning of communism, clearly functions as a teaching moment in her text. In recapitulating Kennedy's explanation (81), rendered in deliberately lay terms, Brown offers an opportunity for her reader's vicarious edification. Although Kennedy is the catalyst for Brown's political awakening, what she learns over the course of their interaction is also responsible for the eventual dissolution of the relationship. The contradiction presented by her life with Kennedy, along with the restlessness and rage created by her growing political awareness, sets the stage for her eventual attraction to the Black Panther Party. Contrary to the increasing emptiness and insignificance she experiences as Kennedy's mistress, the Party promises to fulfill her longing for a sense of purpose. Brown moves from passively receiving Kennedy's teachings to actively assuming responsibility for her own education when the relationship with him dissolves.

After Jay Kennedy, Brown's friendship with Beverlee marks the next major critical point in her evolving political consciousness. Brown remembers initially resisting and even taking offense to Beverlee's assumed familiarity in addressing her as "sister," as Beverlee introduced her to resources that encouraged the development of her critical literacy. Brown writes: "Beverlee was relentless and too smart for me, armed though I was with Jay's lessons. She spat out to me the words of Malcolm X, Langston Hughes, Ralph Ellison, and Richard Wright" (A Taste, 99). In addition to acquainting Brown with the girls in the Jordan housing project, Beverlee also introduced her to Tommy Jacquette, the first real (meaning racially and politically conscious) "Black man," Brown recalls, that she ever knew (105). Encouraged by Jacquette to attend a meeting of the Black Congress in Watts, Brown eventually became active in the organization. Brown explains that the Black Congress was a coalition of several different groups whose executive committee consisted of one representative each from the National Welfare Rights Organization, the Black Panther Political Party (headed by John Floyd), the Community Alert Patrol, and US (founded by Ron Karenga). Brown continued her education after work and between involvement in campus activities by, as she attests, "reading and studying . . . black literature and revolutionary treatises—particularly works like Frantz Fanon's *Wretched of the Earth*—at night" (112). Later, when she became a member of the BPP, the push for critical literacy intensified. New Party recruits, Brown writes, were expected to familiarize themselves with the writings of Mikhail Bakunin, Che Guevara, Mao Zedong, and Karl Marx, among others (137).[2]

While Brown's education for critical literacy began under Jay Kennedy's tutelage, Shakur was introduced to the meaning of American imperialism, socialism, and communism through repeated off-campus encounters with a group of politically astute African students attending Columbia University. Shakur remembers her initial resistance to the idea of communism even though she had no genuine understanding of the economic system the term denoted. She recalls: "When someone asked me what communism was, i opened my mouth to answer, then realized i didn't have the faintest idea. My image of a communist came from a cartoon. It was a spy with a black trench coat and a black hat pulled down over his face, slinking around corners. In school, we were taught that communists worked in salt mines, that they weren't free, that everybody wore the same clothes, and that no one owned anything. The Africans rolled with laughter" (*Assata*, 151). Shakur marvels at the extent of her own brainwashing, recognizing the absurdity of having been adamantly opposed to something about which she had no understanding. In encouraging her to challenge her own cultural assumptions

---

[2] In "Sister Act: Symbol and Substance in Black Women's Leadership," Kathleen Cleaver disputes the inclusion of Marx among the Party's early list of required readings (K. Cleaver, 97).

and ways of knowing, the African students offered Shakur important tools toward developing critical literacy. Relating the way in which her own consciousness was transformed, she encourages her reader to engage in similar self-critique. She concludes: "It's got to be one of the most basic principles of living: always decide who your enemies are for yourself, and never let your enemies choose your enemies for you" (152). Importantly, Shakur indicates that she also learned from Black people who were knowledgeable not only from reading but from actually participating in struggle (175). She says of herself: "i knew i didn't want to be an intellectual, spending my life in books and libraries without knowing what the hell was going on in the streets. Theory without practice is just as incomplete as practice without theory" (180). Repeatedly, her text underscores this imperative of merging theory with practice. As part of her efforts toward self-education, Shakur, like Brown and Davis, studied the dynamics of movements against colonial domination in Africa as well as the theoretical writings of other revolutionaries. From the works of Che Guevara, Carlos Mariguella, and the Tupararos (197), she learned vital information about guerrilla warfare and clandestine struggle. She further acknowledges that exposure to this material was probably what saved her life during the years she was forced underground (198).

Although Davis, Shakur, and Brown attempt to theorize many aspects of their early experiences in a way that self-consciously reveals the birth and development of each writer's revolutionary consciousness, there is notably one issue about which each woman remains relatively silent. This silence concerns the quality of each woman's relationship with her birth family leading up to and through her involvement in radical political struggle. While some of these silences are undoubtedly strategic— meant, for instance, to protect the safety of their families, the welfare of other activists or the integrity of the struggle—there are other silences that seem to fall outside such considerations. If we speak of these texts collectively as modeling the process or processes by which Black women move into radical subjectivity, then such silences have potentially significant implications. It seems worthwhile to examine, by way of closure, what some of these implications are.

During the question-and-answer period following her April 19, 1994, lecture at Cornell University, I asked former Black Panther Kathleen

Cleaver how her (middle-class) family had initially responded to her earlier activism. In a manner that seemed to discourage further inquiry, she replied tersely: "They didn't like it." In the spirit of Cleaver's comment, discussion of potential conflict with and resistance from their respective families (mostly out of the family's understandable concern for their safety and welfare) is for the most part elided from Black Power activists' stories. Readers of George Jackson's epistolary *Soledad Brother* will remember, for instance, the way this collection of letters unfolds to reveal the psychological transformation his parents (and particularly his mother, Georgia Jackson) undergo in coming to terms with his status as a political prisoner. By contrast, Davis, Brown, and Shakur leave this potentially painful aspect of their respective struggles largely unarticulated. Perhaps Jackson's isolation in prison and resulting inability to cultivate alternative support systems (i.e., to compensate for ideological alienation from his birth family) is responsible for the considerable concern and anxiety he registers in his letters over his family's expressions of understanding, approval or disapproval. For Davis, Brown, and Shakur, this need for familial support is perhaps satisfied in part by their other associations. Shakur, for example, pays notable tribute to an extensive network of friends and other activists. Like Brown, who found a family among other activists residing at Camelot (the name given Ericka and John Huggins's apartment, which became a hub of activity for the southern California branch of the Party), Shakur spent a good deal of time both working alongside and living communally with other activists, such that even the meaning of *family* is redefined.

Brown and Davis share the fact that prior to their own activism, they each had parents involved in political work. Brown mentions that before she was born, her mother was involved in union organizing among factory workers. She writes that Dorothy Clark, along with her brother Grant (Brown's uncle) "and their friends would come together in political discussion groups, like thousands of other blacks in America at the time, seeing hope in Moscow's embrace, idealistically seeking any means to right centuries of wrong" (*A Taste*, 322). Similarly, Davis notes that her parents' activism preceded her own. As a college student, her mother had been involved in antiracist movements including the famous Scottsboro case (*Autobiography*, 79). Furthermore, Davis notes that her family was, in 1948, also the first Black family to integrate the neighborhood in which she grew up. The violence with which their arrival and that of subsequent Black families was greeted resulted in the residents' renaming the neighborhood "Dynamite Hill." Sallye Davis's support for Angela and her active involvement in the international campaign to secure her release from prison are described in depth in Bettina Aptheker's *The Morning Breaks*. Aptheker indicates that Sallye Davis "defended the Scottsboro Boys and Angelo Herndon and the Martinsville Seven and Willie McGee before some of us were even born. Thirty years ago she was fighting jim crow in Alabama" (Aptheker, 103). Noting the ironic parallels between her own life and her mother's, Davis recently confessed: "It took me a long time to recognize that I was actually living out my mother's legacy, because I always saw myself as challenging her and doing what she did not" (Cleaver and Davis, 160). Sallye Davis's own history of activism notwithstanding, Davis maintains that her mother, like Cleaver's family, was nevertheless "quite upset" upon learning of Davis's work with the Black Panther Party (Cleaver and Davis, 160).

While Davis and Shakur indicate that their families were ultimately supportive during the most critical moments in their ordeals, there is little indication that the change might have been the result of a painful and/or protracted process. Whatever resistance the women may have encountered from their families initially is perhaps recast by their reading of earlier periods through present awareness. Because George Jackson's narrative, by contrast, is epistolary, this is precisely the prerogative he is denied. Acknowledging his mother's transformation into an activist in her own right, Jackson makes a plea to Joan Hammer—a member of the Soledad Defense Committee—to remove from the final manuscript all of his earlier criticisms about his mother. He beseeches: "Go over all the letters I've sent you, any reference to Georgia being less than a perfect revolutionary's mama must be removed. Do it now! I want no possibility of anyone misunderstanding her as I did" (Jackson, *Soledad*, 247). In detailing only the beginning and the end, Davis and Shakur leave out the middle that Jackson's text (inadvertently—if his wishes had been actualized) poignantly captures. Shakur is vague about the details of conflicts during her teen years with her mother and stepfather. Her narrative focuses more on her reaction (emotional distancing) to her family than on the specific details of her conflicts with them. In response to her rebelliousness, her mother, she writes, "would talk to me, slap me, shake me, punish me, but nothing worked. I was a lost cause. I was running away from home and i didn't even know it" (*Assata*, 74). This notion of running away from home is resonant for its symbolic as well as its literal significance. Running away from home is not just about running away from one's family, but also about leaving behind the security of what is familiar or known. The psychic impact of such dislocation, however, is only cursorily explored. There is little information to suggest *how* Shakur moved from this early period of conflict with her mother to reconciliation during the later years of her most intense activism. By the time of her capture on the New Jersey Turnpike and subsequent hospitalization, this rift apparently had been mended. Shakur writes of receiving her mother's unconditional support at her hospital bedside. When her mother tells her that she is proud of her, Shakur writes: "The words spin around me, weaving a warm blanket of love. I am so happy. I can hardly contain myself. My mother is proud of me. She loves me and she is proud of me" (16). The fact that the revelation is so important to Shakur suggests the possibility of tension in their relationship prior to this reunion. The nature of the reconciliation with her mother seems to be captured best in a sixteen-stanza poem in which Shakur expresses compassion toward her mother as a result of being able to look back with new understanding of how oppression affected their relationship (193). She finally understands as an adult and an activist what she could not as a teen: that her mother sought to protect her in the only ways she knew how. Shakur writes good-humoredly, "She knows that i am half crazy" (196). Long before Shakur herself, the mother recognized the daughter's capacity to get herself killed. It is not mental instability but the spirit of resistance which makes one "(half) crazy" in a society where consistent challenges to authority are met with increasing repression. "Craziness" is, in fact, a recurring trope in African American literature and culture. The individual labeled "crazy" is the one whose audacity and apparent fearlessness inspire awe (or dread) and whose actions consistently defy others' expectations. In the end, Shakur suggests that her mother, like Davis's and Jackson's, is moved by having witnessed the state's abuses of power in its efforts to apprehend her daughter.

Brown's interest in and involvement with the Panthers left her mother baffled over her daughter's seemingly sudden plunge into blackness after their joint effort for so many years to escape it. "My mother," she comments, "with whom I still lived, thought I was insane" (*A Taste*, 121). Most of the narrative attention Davis, Shakur, and Brown devote to their families is before and after the fact of their activism. In different ways, each expresses concern over the stress to which their families were subjected as a result of their political activities. Brown, for example, expresses regret over the financial hardship her mother endured in order to raise her bail after an arrest (174). With respect to her parents, Davis writes: "I knew they would not bend under the terrible pressures to denounce their 'Communist daughter.' At the same time I realized that the more strongly they defended me, the more their own safety would be placed in jeopardy; I worried a great deal about them" (*Autobiography*, 221). Noting that her flight into exile brought tremendous police and FBI surveillance and harassment to bear on her family, Shakur's narrative, like Jackson's letters, points to the way the older generation can be radicalized by the activism of their children. When they begin to witness and experience firsthand the same intense repression visited on their children, their consciousness is inevitably altered. Reminiscent of the sentiment expressed in her poem "Story," Shakur notes that her family had not only survived the experience but had "grown stronger in the process" (*Assata*, 273). Out of their own victimization and rage, they are better able to understand the reasons for and importance of their children's involvement in resistance struggle. In this way, they, too, are ultimately drawn into struggle. Georgia Jackson, in fact, in agitating on behalf of her son George and other political prisoners, eventually becomes—as Davis's narrative also attests—an activist in her own right (*Autobiography*, 254). Cognizant of the suffering and sacrifices endured on their behalf by their respective families, Davis and Shakur, in writing their autobiographies, may have succumbed to the same kind of romantic revisionism (with regard to portraying their relationships with family) that Jackson might have carried out had he exercised final editorial control.

On a strategic level, the desire to protect their families from further harassment and invasion of privacy might provide another explanation for why the activists choose not to explore or recount personal intrafamilial conflicts as part of their narratives. To disclose the nature of past struggles with their families after such wounds may have been either healed or forgiven could inflict unnecessary pain, possibly even guilt or embarrassment, on family members still surviving. It could also contribute to further alienation and isolation of the activists themselves. If, on the other hand, such silences are unconscious, they might be read as marking trauma still too painful to revisit. And since all three women cultivate additional support systems through which they receive affirmation for their beliefs, values, and political commitment, there is less need to focus on the responses of their birth families. The women essentially redefine the meaning of family to extend beyond the narrow definition of blood relations. The term comes to include all those who provide emotional as well as material sustenance and support.

In keeping with other objectives of their texts, though, perhaps the most compelling reason for the silences around family may be that they enable the continued focusing of attention on the repression of the state rather than on the particular dynamics within individual families. If families sometimes inadvertently act as agents of repression (i.e., in reproducing the values and interests of the state[3]), clearly the women are interested in locating the *source* of such repression in the practices and ideology of the culture as a whole. Refusing to air personal conflicts with their respective families also avoids vindicating the opposition. Since the aim of the state is always to undermine—or if possible, dismantle—all potential support networks available to political dissidents, detailing intrafamilial conflict would simply prove that the methods of the state had been effective. One unfortunate consequence, however, of the elision of this struggle from their stories is that, from a pedagogical standpoint, it is a lost opportunity to share what sorts of strategies enable women to overcome the stress and strain of intense conflict with those we love. How does one mend or maintain relations with family while continuing political work if the latter are ideologically or practically opposed to one's participation in such activity? Finally, in contrast to Jackson's text, there is no opportunity to actually witness the dialogical and dialectical process through which an entire family becomes radicalized by the activities of an individual member. In taking up such questions, these three women's texts might have contributed valuable insight to feminist theorizing about the nature of women's transitions from the private to the public sphere.

---

[3] See Wilhelm Reich, *The Mass Psychology of Fascism*; bell hooks, *Talking Back: Thinking Feminist, Thinking Black*; Michel Foucault, *Power/Knowledge* and *Discipline & Punish*.

Chapter 4

Autobiography as Political/Personal Intervention

Like other writers of resistance narratives, Davis, Shakur, and Brown fashion autobiographies that are extensions of their political work. A salient characteristic of resistance narratives is the challenge they pose to hegemonic history. In writing their lives, activists seek to document their experiences, to correct misinformation, to educate their readers, and to encourage the continuation of struggle. As Barbara Harlow has noted: "The connection between knowledge and power, the awareness of the exploitation of knowledge by the interests of power to create a distorted historical record, is central to resistance narratives" (Harlow, *Resistance*, 116). Harlow further asserts that the struggle to control the historical record is "seen from all sides as no less crucial than the armed struggle" (7). Although Harlow's work to date has focused largely on international liberation struggles waged by organizations like the Palestine Liberation Organization, the Sandinista National Liberation Front (Nicaragua), and the African National Congress (South Africa), to name only a few, the observations she makes are often applicable to Black Power activists in the United States as well.

Davis's, Shakur's, and Brown's challenge to hegemonic ways of knowing includes not only their rewriting the distorted American history they were fed as part of their formal schooling (discussed in chapter 3), but also their revising the history of the Movement itself. In the women's texts, revising Movement history takes place on two levels. On one level, they, like other activists (male and female), seek to provide that side of the story silenced or distorted in hegemonic accounts of the period. Because History is traditionally written from the vantage point of the victor and not the vanquished, activists who write autobiography aim to fill in or recast important information about key events or issues in the struggle that have been elided in the dominant accounts of the period. On another level, writing autobiography also affords activists one means of recuperating their own public image. On this level, the women manage to revise their individual histories within the story of the Movement. In this chapter I examine the multiple levels of political intervention at work in Davis's, Shakur's, and Brown's narratives: specifically, their rewriting of Movement history, their conscientious manipulation of language to foster alternative/counterhegemonic ways of seeing and knowing, and their reinventing of self as a sometimes self-conscious but always inevitable outcome of the autobiographical process.

Perhaps one of the most notable instances of the writers' use of their texts to challenge the dominant historical record is the counter-history all three women forge around young Jonathan Jackson's siege of a Marin County courtroom on August 7, 1970. The siege ostensibly was to demand the release of Jon's brother, George, along with other political prisoners. For many activists of the Movement, the young Jackson's act was revered as heroic. In the autobiographies of the period, he becomes a legend. In her narrative, for example, Shakur marvels over Jackson: "Seventeen years old and taking freedom into his own hands. Seventeen years old and defying the whole pig power structure in amerika. Seventeen years old and dead. . . . Who was the young man who came to free a revolutionary Black prisoner, holding a district attorney and a pig judge hostage, shouting, 'We are the revolutionaries! Free the Soledad Brothers by 12:30'?" (*Assata*, 206). Shakur's repetition of Jackson's tender age captures her sense of awe and praise for his bravery. She further notes that the news of the siege became a defining moment in her desire to become a revolutionary (207). Inspired by Jackson's courage, Shakur writes: "If i stay a victim it will kill me, i thought. It was time for me to get my shit together. I wanted to be one of the people who stood up. These were serious times" (206).

Davis, who was personally acquainted with Jonathan and the Jackson family through her work with the Soledad Defense Committee, offers a detailed portrait of the young Jackson as a politically astute, precocious, and extremely serious young man, who was wholeheartedly committed to his brother's defense (*Autobiography*, 265–68). Like Shakur, Davis indicates that Jackson's death merely renewed her commitment to resistance struggle. She writes: "I knew that there was only one way to avenge

Jon's death—through struggle, political struggle, through people in motion, fighting for all those behind walls" (279). Of course, Jackson's siege was also a pivotal moment in Davis's life because Jackson's use of weapons legally registered in her name made her the target of a massive FBI woman-hunt immediately following the takeover. Her autobiography opens with news of Jackson's siege and her subsequent flight as a fugitive from (in)justice. Reluctant to treat the takeover alone as a *revolutionary* act, Davis focuses instead on the context and larger significance of Jackson's revolt. In the wake of his death, she writes: "Now the enemy had closed in on Jon, who had tried to make some dent in the formidable prison system which was turning his brother—all his brothers and sisters—around and around, faster and faster in a vicious orbit of misery and brutality, frame-ups and assassinations" (279). Elsewhere, Davis refers to Jackson's act as an understandable expression of deep frustration over having witnessed repeated injustice directed toward his brother and other political prisoners (367). Davis's careful wording reflects the ensuing uncertainty surrounding Jackson's exact intentions. The testimony of eyewitnesses, who claimed to have heard one of the prisoners demand the release of the Soledad Brothers (i.e., George Jackson, Fleeta Drumgo, and John Clutchette, who were all incarcerated in Soledad Prison) as he fled the courthouse, was used by prosecutors in the attempt to construct a motive. However, not only was there conflicting testimony around exactly what was said and by whom as the prisoners fled the building with the hostages, but as the defense noted, "Free the Soledad Brothers" was a slogan with enormous currency at the time, and so did not necessarily constitute the prisoners' immediate purpose in taking hostages. In her narrative, Davis notes that a letter written to her by Ruchell Magee in the aftermath of the incident indicated that the takeover had not been to demand the release of the Soledad Brothers, but to gain access to a radio station, "where they could expose to the world the railroads so many of them had received instead of trials, the incredibly wretched conditions of their existence behind walls and, in particular, the recent murder by San Quentin guards of a prisoner named Fred Billingslea" (369). The circumstances surrounding Billingslea's death are recounted at length in Bettina Aptheker's *The Morning Breaks* (Aptheker, 187–200).

Brown's memory of Jackson is similarly of a serious and deeply reflective young man. She recalls: "I thought he was too serious most of the time, though he was only seventeen years old" (*A Taste*, 218). Brown learned of Jackson's death while in Vietnam as part of a Panther delegation led by Eldridge Cleaver. She recalls reading details of the incident in a translated French-language edition of *Newsweek* (229). Later, her recounting of his violent death is, like Shakur's and Brown's, suffused with a stunning sense of loss, though less personal than collective. The recasting of Jackson's act from criminal to heroic by means of supplying a social and political context for the act (something rigorously suppressed by mainstream media) underscores the writers' shared engagement with redefining the meaning of criminality. By foregrounding the imbalance of power between America's haves and have-nots and by insisting upon the relevance of such to the dispensation of justice, the writers directly challenge the validity of a legal and economic system that implicitly denies the right (and "moral imperative") of oppressed people to actively resist their exploitation. In the process, the state is exposed as the original architect of violence and repression, while the people's resistance is reclaimed as healthy, reasonable, and just.

Even as the precise details and exact sequence of events surrounding the Marin County courtroom takeover and its dramatic aftermath remain unclear, the meaning of Jon Jackson's life is rescued from obscurity by inclusion of the incident, and its alleged significance to the larger struggle, in other activists' narratives. Among the information that otherwise often conflicting accounts *do* agree on is that at some point during the trial of James McClain (for the March 2, 1970, stabbing of San Quentin Prison guard E. K. Irwin), Jonathan Jackson, armed, stood up in the courtroom and, aided by the three San Quentin prisoners present, seized several hostages in a takeover that was ultimately crushed. Besides McClain, the other two prisoners involved were Ruchell Magee and William Christmas (referred to as "Arthur Christmas" in Brown's narrative—*A Taste*, 230). In the end, Jackson, Judge Haley, Christmas, and McClain were fatally shot, while Deputy District Attorney Gary Thomas, Magee, and some jurors were seriously wounded. The account of the incident recorded in Davis's narrative indicates that the first shot that precipitated the exchange of fire came from a San Quentin guard who fired on the van as it attempted to drive away. This version is corroborated by an article appearing in the *San Francisco Examiner*, which proposed that "the tragic shoot-out which took four lives at Marin County's Civic Center Friday was triggered by two San Quentin guards who didn't hear an order not to shoot" (Hatfield, 1). The article further notes that Judge Haley was fatally wounded immediately after the first two shots; it was following these shots that Thomas managed to wrest the gun from Jackson and to shoot at three of his captors.

Yet another article appearing the following day in the *Examiner* indicated that San Quentin guard John Matthews was probably the first officer to fire at the van. Matthews maintains that he fired after two guns allegedly were aimed at him and one actually discharged. He further indicated that he returned the fire that likely killed the driver (Waite, 20). Although in writing about the incident in her autobiography, Brown had the advantage of greater objective historical distance, her remembering of the incident does not seem concerned with resolving earlier conflicting accounts. Rather, she simply adds another version to the existing lore. Contrary to Davis, who writes that a single San Quentin guard firing on the van precipitated a "barrage of shots [which] tore into the van" (*Autobiography*, 278), Brown asserts that "*hundreds and hundreds of rounds* from the weapons of San Quentin guards and sharp-shooters" were sprayed into the van the moment its occupants were aboard (*A Taste*, 230; emphasis added). She also writes that Jackson's body, recovered in the driver's seat, had been "riddled with bullets."

In another article appearing in the August 8, 1970, *San Francisco Chronicle*, evidence is offered to suggest that the initial shots may have come from *inside* the van (Popp, 1). In the wake of the shooting, Gary Thomas is said to have told District Attorney Bruce Bales that while he [Thomas] was inside the van, he managed to wrest away the driver's gun and to shoot several of the captors. He allegedly declared: "I got three of them [the gunmen] and I hope I killed them. I grabbed a gun from the driver" (14). Several witnesses similarly noted that the first shots fired seemed to have sounded from within the van.

In the end, authorities determined that at least four shots were fired from within the van, and six or more were fired into it from the outside (clearly a contrast to the "hundreds and hundreds of rounds" Brown's retelling of the incident proposes). Finally, the article in the *Examiner* maintains that McClain was the driver of the truck, while the *Chronicle* states that Jackson's body was the one found slumped over the wheel.

This discrepancy is explained by Bettina Aptheker, who notes that Jackson took over the wheel from McClain after the van stalled and McClain was unable to restart it (Aptheker, 191). What is most intriguing about the various newspaper articles on the incident, however, is that the focus is consistently and almost exclusively on McClain, Magee, and Christmas as common criminals with long histories within the criminal justice system. Only scant attention is given to the presence, role, and possible motives of Jackson (who, incidentally, had no previous criminal record), although he appears prominently in photographs taken during the siege. A photo accompanying the cover story in the August 9, 1970, *Examiner*, for instance, shows Jackson armed with two guns, leading the way out of the courtroom. The mainstream media's coverage of the event effectively silenced alternative readings which might have brought to bear other relevant issues such as the routine brutalization of prisoners in San Quentin (of which Magee was a victim), the denial of fair trials to those economically underprivileged, and the reality of racism in judicial sentencing. The mainstream media's coverage of the Marin County courtroom revolt is thus reread in the texts of Davis, Shakur, and Brown in a manner that creates a counternarrative to the dominant historical record. In their texts, both Jackson himself and the significance of his act are recovered from potential obscurity.

Another important rereading of a major event in the process of creating an alternative or counter-history is found in Brown's retelling of the FBI-engineered assassinations of Black Panther activists Fred Hampton and Mark Clark on December 4, 1969. The murders, which are also mentioned by Davis (*Autobiography*, 226) and Shakur (*Assata*, 52), are treated with the most detail in Brown's narrative. Hampton, the twenty-one-year-old chairman of the Illinois chapter of the BPP, was considered controversial and threatening primarily because of his efforts to organize members of the Blackstone Rangers (one of Chicago's most powerful Black gangs) into political activism with the BPP. Kenneth O'Reilly notes that Hampton was well known as "a charismatic and skilled organizer who formed a shaky alliance with SDS, organized a number of community welfare, medical, and educational programs, and somehow kept the rivalry with the Blackstone Rangers in check" (O'Reilly, 311). In retelling the story of Hampton's assassination, Brown indicates that Hampton's partner, Deborah Johnson (at the time eight and a half months pregnant with their child), was unable to awaken Hampton the night the police raided their home. Brown writes: "Dozens of bullets from Thompson submachine guns had been pumped into his bed, two bullets fired point-blank into his head. It had been an FBI assassination under the direction of special agent Marlin Johnson, carried out by Illinois state police wielding twenty-seven guns and led by their nigger, James 'Gloves' Davis" (A Taste, 206).[1] Arriving for the funeral five days after the assassination, Brown recalls that she touched the bed and found it still soaking wet with Hampton's blood (205). Brown does not mention the late William O'Neal, now known as the FBI infiltrator who, entrusted with Panther security for the Chicago branch, is believed to have drugged Hampton with secobarbital the night of the murder. Despite official claims that a gun battle ensued, ballistic reports revealed that all but one of the more than ninety shots fired in Hampton's Monroe Street home came from the police (Eyes on the Prize). The one bullet fired by Panthers in self-defense came from Mark Clark, who was gunned down with a bullet to the chest during the initial moments of the raid. In the days following the murders, Brown remembers that "thousands of people were lined up to look inside, at the place where 'Chairman Fred,' as he was known all over Black Chicago, had been assassinated. The chapter wanted black people to see, to know the extent to which the police would go to repress resistance to their oppression" (A Taste, 205). In the two weeks before the police finally cordoned off the site, the Panthers conducted tours for people in the community so that they, too, could bear witness. Brown's decision to retell the incident in her autobiography is likewise an act of bearing witness. By countering disinformation and filling in the silences left by the mass media, Brown, like Davis and Shakur, uses her narrative to teach in the project of educating for critical literacy.

This goal of educating for critical literacy is perhaps most apparent in Davis's and Shakur's presentation of their respective court trials. In recounting their trials, both women launch salient critiques of U.S. do-

---

[1] James "Gloves" Davis is identified as "Phillip Joseph 'Gloves' Davis" by Ward Churchill and Jim Vander Wall (Agents of Repression, 66). However, Kenneth O'Reilly corroborates Brown's identification of him as James "Gloves" Davis (O'Reilly, 311).

mestic policy as it affects poor people of color in particular, and of corruption within the U.S. criminal justice system. Their experiences offer countertestimony that challenges conventional ways of knowing and that—by bringing forth the voices of those marginalized and/or silenced by the policies of the dominant culture—encourages a reexamination of the relation between ideology, authority, and power.

Through recounting their trials, Shakur and Davis are able not only to offer an alternative reading that explains and contextualizes the political activity in which they were involved, but also to expose the corruption within the U.S. justice system. While Davis focuses on the single trial stemming from the Marin County courtroom takeover in August 1970, Shakur's narrative incorporates her experiences defending charges in jury trials arising from four separate incidents from 1971 to 1973: a bank robbery in Queens, New York, on August 23, 1971; a bank robbery in Bronx, New York, on September 1, 1972; the kidnapping of a drug dealer on December 28, 1972; and the fatal shooting of Werner Foerster, a New Jersey state trooper, on May 2, 1973. Like many political prisoners, Shakur was indicted and prosecuted largely on manufactured evidence and perjured testimony. Although all of the other judgments against her were either dismissed or overturned, she was ultimately convicted in March 1977 of Foerster's death. While Davis was eventually (after two years) acquitted of all charges against her, her trial experiences nevertheless shed light on the difficulty for Black people, particularly political prisoners, of securing a hearing that even approximates justice.

Because jury selection is critical in any trial, considerable attention is given to the voir dire process in both Davis's and Shakur's texts. Each highlights the fact that justice is already compromised for Black defendants in that potential jurors are traditionally selected from county voting rolls. Since, as Shakur points out, the interests of poor people and of Blacks are seldom represented by candidates running for political office, this faction of the population is less inclined to participate in voter registration (*Assata*, 118). The consequence is that Black defendants like Davis and Shakur are denied, de facto, the likelihood of assembling a jury of their peers. For this reason, the voir dire process—the opportunity to challenge individual jurors before they are seated—was especially critical to their cases. Davis reproduces, in her narrative, many of the responses elicited from individual jurors during the voir dire in order to illustrate the success of state propaganda in turning people against ideas and concepts they do not necessarily understand. Although few jurors could define (except in tautological terms) what a *communist* was, for example, Davis notes that all revealed strong antipathy toward the term itself (*Autobiography*, 355), and therefore a predisposition to judge her guilty. Shakur is likewise attentive to the role of the state and the media in creating and shaping public opinion. In the same way that Davis must face potential jurors' preconceived notions about communism based on national propaganda, Shakur confronts the mass media-induced hysteria and distortions around the composition and activities of the Black Liberation Army. For both, one of the primary challenges is to demystify their respective struggles in a way that allows people outside to understand the issues at stake. Furthermore, when Davis and Shakur are allowed to speak for themselves, the fact that they are intelligent, logical, and articulate undermines the state's capacity to deny their humanity.

Like the voir dire, the opening statement from both Davis's and Shakur's trials is an important pedagogical moment in their respective narratives. Davis participates in her own defense by delivering a two-hour-long opening statement to the jury which is excerpted in the autobiography (*Autobiography*, 367). Of the portions she includes, perhaps the most noteworthy is her challenge to the prosecution's claim that hers was a crime of passion. Astutely, Davis accuses the prosecution of sexism in assuming passion for George Jackson as the motive underlying her political activism and her alleged conspiracy with his brother, Jon, to free the Soledad Brothers. Ironically, prosecutor Albert Harris's attempt to lift Davis's politically charged comments out of context and to place undue emphasis on particular word choices backfires. The state's case against her is undermined as the content of the letter reveals a feminist, activist sensibility clearly incompatible with Harris's charges. The supposed "love letter" from Davis to Jackson defends women's role in the struggle and argues for the necessity of revisioning gender role expectations that do not serve the interests of liberation (371). Because of the prosecution's misguided strategy, Barbara Harlow has noted that Davis's trial (along with her acquittal) "was as much a defense of a woman's specific role in the struggle as it was a critique of the United States judicial apparatus" (Harlow, *Barred*, 194). Davis's inclusion of the trial as part of her narrative effectively illustrates the flimsiness of the prosecution's case against her, and also exposes the political nature of the state's persecution, since she is detained nearly two years without bail based on insubstantial evidence.

Significantly, Davis also uses the circumstances of her trial to raise again the issue of class. While she neglects earlier in the narrative to focus on class privilege in terms of the unique *educational* opportunities it potentially affords, Davis never attempts to obscure the *fact* of her own class privilege. Cognizant of the ways such difference can be and usually is manipulated by power to discourage solidarity across class lines, Davis reaffirms connection to the most dispossessed of American society in her treatment of Ruchell Magee, her codefendant until their cases were eventually severed. Davis resists the attempts of others to separate her from people like Magee (i.e., poor, Black, illiterate, and otherwise disenfranchised individuals) by their focus on her relatively privileged background. Davis indicates that the media repeatedly sought to contrast her with Magee, who was painted as a loathsome common criminal whose resistance was situated in a context of Black monstrosity rather than revolutionary desire. Davis avoids capitulating to a strategy of divide and conquer by reinforcing her and Magee's shared spirit of resistance to racist oppression. Instead of setting herself apart from Magee, Davis highlights the issue of class injustice and subsequently places their respective acts of resistance along a continuum of justifiable and appropriate responses to oppressive conditions based on the particular social, political, and economic milieu within which each, through no fault of their own, is situated.

Shakur's recapitulation of her trials is similarly suffused with important pedagogical moments. As she delivers her opening statement at the trial for the alleged kidnapping of a drug dealer, Shakur's education of the jury is also an education of her readers. She begins by noting that hers will not be a "conventional opening statement," but that it will attempt to situate her actions and the charges against her in an emphatically political context (*Assata*, 166). This context includes the particular social and economic circumstances motivating and necessitating resistance struggle, the mainstream media's distortion of information about her and about the Movement, and the government's long, documented history of repression against political dissidents. Shakur cites as examples

Marcus Garvey, Stokely Carmichael, Angela Davis, the Rosenbergs, Lolita Lebrón, and Martin Luther King Jr. (167). As with her Independence Day address ("To My People, July 4, 1973"), Shakur prompts the jurors/reader to consider the way those in power co-opt language to serve their own interests. The true "criminals" in a society, Shakur argues, are not those who steal a box of Pampers to clothe an infant, but heads of state and CEOs of powerful corporations who have been known to oversee the devastation of entire communities of people in the name of war or profit. By redefining criminality, among other things, Shakur draws attention to the way language shapes our understanding of reality. Her address to the jury is essentially an exercise in deconstruction; binary oppositions, such as good/bad, criminal/lawful, dangerous/benign, just/unjust, as established by the state in setting itself against political activists, are all inverted through Shakur's analyses. In the end, Shakur (like countless Black activists as far back as the late eighteenth century) seizes upon the state's own terms—significantly, the text of the Declaration of Independence—to create psychic dissonance in her audience. Either political resistance in the face of oppression is legitimate or the country's reverence for the Declaration's tenets is hypocritical. By using something well-known, Shakur endeavors to help her audience conceptualize an unknown.

Shakur's retelling of her court trials charts her increasing disillusionment with the possibility of political prisoners being treated fairly within the system. Initially she is sanguine, believing that once the defense is allowed to state its case, the rules of logic alone will ensure her vindication for crimes she did not commit. However, a series of circumstances—from the precariousness of the voir dire process, to the corruptibility of trial judges, to the state's capacity to manufacture evidence when all else fails—rapidly erodes her optimism. Shakur's text explodes the myth of fair trials for poor/political prisoners on several counts. Not only is her defense team financially unable to absorb the cost of securing the experts needed to counter testimony offered by the state's expert witnesses, they also are unable to find specialists willing to risk their careers by testifying on behalf of such a controversial defendant (Assata, 245). As Shakur's aunt and attorney, Evelyn Williams, corroborates in her autobiography, Inadmissible Evidence, the fact that Shakur was accused of killing a cop meant that most of the forensic and ballistic specialists they approached declined on the grounds of conflict of interest since they not only routinely performed work for law enforcement outfits, but counted on maintaining that business for their livelihood.

In the Bronx bank robbery trial, Shakur was prevented from launching an appropriate defense by the judge, who forced the case to trial before the lawyers had been allotted adequate time to prepare. In protest, Shakur and Kamau, her codefendant, decided to have their lawyers remain mute while they assumed their own defense. Rejecting the dictates of courtroom decorum, they proceeded to educate the jury about the circumstances of their case. Foremost, they stressed that Judge Gagliardi's ordering the case to trial had compromised their ability to mount a defense. When Shakur and Kamau were repeatedly cited for contempt and eventually barred from the courtroom altogether, the trial, which continued in their absence, was exposed as a complete mockery of justice. Shakur notes that she and Kamau had come to refer to the whole trial as a "vaudeville show" (93). Even Evelyn was eventually cited for contempt after she walked out in protest, having been denied the means of representing her client and therefore rendered superfluous to the proceedings. The trial culminated in a hung jury. When the case was subsequently retried, Shakur and Kamau were acquitted.

Other instances undermining Shakur's right to a fair trial included a judge's order, in the Queens bank robbery trial, that she submit to a photo shoot by the FBI. Convinced that the outcome could be manipulated to convict her unjustly, Shakur explains: "someone had told me about some trick the FBI uses. They take a photo of you in the same angle as the bank photo and superimpose a transparency of the bank photo over it" (161). Shakur was eventually beaten and subdued in order that the pictures might be taken against her will. The photos, however, were later ruled inadmissible by a subsequent judge, who determined that Shakur's rights were violated by the manner in which the photos were obtained.

As another impediment to her ability to receive a fair trial, Shakur cites the illegal surveillance of supposedly confidential conferences between defendants and their counsel. During the trial for the murder of the New Jersey state trooper, for instance, defense lawyers discovered that the offices they were using to meet in were bugged (248). Kenneth O'Reilly writes further that it was not uncommon for the FBI to employ infiltrators in cases of political prisoners to undermine lawyer-client confidentiality. Infiltrator William O'Neal, for example, was known to have provided privileged information to the prosecution by reporting to the FBI on the strategies being used by the lawyers for the families of Fred Hampton and Mark Clark (O'Reilly, 312). Finally, Shakur indicates that the routine harassment of her defense team lawyers by hostile/partial judges also undermined the prospect of her receiving a fair trial. Shakur charges that "[Judge] Appleby's strategy was to completely intimidate the lawyers, to harass them, threaten them until they became fearful of mounting any significant opposition to the legal lynching that was supposed to be my trial" (*Assata*, 248).

Perhaps the most blatant abuses of Shakur's rights as a defendant under the law occur during the trial in which she stood accused of Foerster's May 2, 1973, shooting death on the New Jersey Turnpike. One of the most ominous examples of the vulnerability of political prisoners and their advocates concerns the mysterious circumstances surrounding defense attorney Stanley Cohen's death just days before this scheduled trial. Especially significant is the fact that police seized all of Cohen's legal notes from his apartment following his death. Despite defense motions to regain possession of the papers, most of the notes related to their trial strategy were never recovered (*Assata*, 247). Later, when the defense team's headquarters in New Brunswick were burglarized, and several papers relating to Shakur's case again "rummaged through and stolen," the presiding Judge Appelby refused to honor the defense's motion for an investigation into the incident (251).

The trial for Foerster's death is also one of the few times Shakur excerpts dialogue from the actual court transcript illustrating the bias evident in Appleby's handling of the voir dire. After Appleby's seating of the jurors (lawyers were prevented from participating in the preliminary questioning) *and* the defense's exhaustion of their allotted peremptory challenges, the final jury panel, Shakur notes, still included a woman who had identified herself as the girlfriend of a New Jersey state trooper, and two men who acknowledged that they were related to New Jersey state troopers. Despite the obvious conflict of interest therein, Shakur notes that the defense's motions to dismiss these jurors for cause were all denied (250). As a result of her experiences fighting for her life against manifestations of injustice, corruption, and conspiracy, Shakur ultimately determines that since there is no real protection for political prisoners under the law, she cannot continue to work within the law to gain her freedom. Instead, she realizes that she must *take* her freedom by going outside the law (252). In the end, she chastises herself for having even participated in the New Jersey trial that resulted in her conviction. She writes: "By participating, i participated in my own oppression. I should have known better and not lent dignity or credence to that sham" (252).

An interesting omission in Shakur's recounting of her trials is the tension that sometimes surfaced behind the scenes between the defense lawyers in cases where she was being tried as a codefendant. Shakur's silence in these instances seems deliberately aimed at protecting the image and integrity of the struggle. What she says and does not say about developments surrounding the Bronx bank robbery trial is exemplary. While Shakur avoids going into detail about the exact circumstances that precipitated Evelyn Williams's decision to remove herself as Shakur's attorney when the case was retried (in the autobiography, Shakur maintains merely that they could not agree on trial strategy), more information is provided in Williams's autobiography. In *Inadmissible Evidence*, Williams maintains that the issue was treachery on the part of Kamau's lawyer, Robert Bloom. According to Williams, Bloom had shown himself more than willing to sacrifice Shakur's welfare if it meant the possibility of exonerating his own client, even though he and Williams were supposedly conducting a *team* defense. Williams writes that, in retrospect, she came to realize that Shakur's refusal to acknowledge Bloom's treachery was not out of disregard for her [Williams's] sound legal reservations, but out of Shakur's desire to "maintain cohesiveness with Kamau," even if it meant sacrificing herself in the process (Williams, 120). Importantly, Shakur's decision to omit mention of the incident from her narrative underscores the extent to which the autobiography is for her an extension of her political struggle. Her silence is an expression of solidarity with other activists despite forces that seek to undermine their unity. Shakur's only comment about the case in the autobiography is that she and Kamau were acquitted on January 28, 1973 (118). In *Inadmissible Evidence*, Williams points out that Shakur's sense of integrity was not always reciprocated by her codefendants. Fellow activist Andrew Jackson, for instance, agreed under FBI coercion to testify against Shakur in exchange for leniency in his own case.

Shakur's and Davis's jury trials reveal the extent to which activists understand the critical relationship between language and power. The words used by political activists in stating their cases acquire the status of weapons in their potential to challenge and destabilize dominant ways of knowing. Activists' conscientious manipulation of language/rhetoric to alter ways of seeing reveals, as radical educator Henry Giroux might say, an appreciation of language as "both a terrain of domination and field of possibility" (Giroux, "Literacy," 154). Language, in the narratives of activists, represents a critical site of struggle. As Kenneth O'Reilly has argued, rhetoric was, in fact, *the* most powerful tool at Black Power activists' disposal (O'Reilly, 295–96).

All political activists who write are aware of the power of words to alter understanding. A perfect illustration of this recognition can be found in what Eldridge Cleaver says about deconstructing the assumptions informing political doublespeak. Challenging the conventional wisdom of a so-called "war on poverty," for instance, Cleaver counters: "What we need in the United States is a *war on the rich* . . . on the system that allows poverty to exist in the midst of all those riches" (Lockwood, 4; emphasis added). Cleaver's rhetorical turn, like Shakur's deconstruction of binary oppositions, is significant because it challenges the terms of debate by relocating agency and by illuminating the source of the problem rather than one of its symptoms. Of course, as Cleaver intends to suggest (and as U.S. domestic policy has at times revealed), the language of a "war on poverty" facilitates the short leap to a war on the poor.

Shakur's attentiveness to language for self-empowerment is evident throughout her narrative. Referring to the Black Panther Party's description of the police as "fascist pigs" (as well as her own repeated use of the epithet in the autobiography), for example, she explains that they referred to them as such "not because [we] believed they were nazis but because of the way they acted in our communities" (*Assata*, 10). Such renaming and reframing is strategic because, in this instance, it facilitates an analysis of the dynamics of power and domination while also making implied connections to other manifestations of state repression across historical and geographic boundaries. The origin of the epithet "pig" to refer to cops is explained by Huey Newton in *Revolutionary Suicide*. After searching for a term that would effectively "control the police by making them see themselves in a new light," Newton indicates that he and others came across a satiric postcard bearing the slogan "Support Your Local Police" with an accompanying illustration of a "grinning, slobbering pig." Newton recalls: "It was just what we were looking for. . . . This was a form of psychological warfare: it raised the consciousness of the people and also inflicted a new consciousness on the ruling circle." Newton further notes that apart from the term's negative social connotation, the epithet "pig" was also ideal because the word itself was racially neutral. It thus had the potential to appeal to many different groups who experienced conflicts with the police. Newton explains: "Many white youths on college campuses began to understand what the police were really like when their heads were broken open during demonstrations against the draft and the Vietnam war. This broadened the use of the term and served to unify the victims against their oppressors" (Newton, *Revolutionary Suicide*, 165–66).

Shakur's attention to the politics of language includes her problematizing of the way the term "liberal" (as invoked, for instance, in the mass media) has come to have no meaning at all except as a safe haven for those unwilling to risk expressing or acting on genuine political conviction. Located ambiguously between the fascist-oriented Right and the socialist-oriented Left, the term, Shakur claims, covers too much territory to represent any serious willingness to stand for anything. She marvels: "I have never really understood exactly what a 'liberal' is. . . . As far as i'm concerned, 'liberal' is the most meaningless word in the dictionary" (*Assata*, 132). Shakur's attention to language is also manifest at the level of form. Her consistent use of lowercase initials for proper names (e.g., amerika, new jersey, kourt, leavenworth), her lowercase rendering of the first-person pronoun (i.e., "i"), and her deliberate alteration of conventional spellings (e.g., substituting the Germanic *k* for the letter *c* in the previous list) point to a subversion of language that better reflects her own particular experience, and simultaneously opens up the possibility of reconsidering old ways of knowing. That is, how might the capitalization of states/of countries help to naturalize (and legitimize) territorialism and governmental aggression by concealing the artificial division of land and resources that arguably should belong to all citizens of the earth? Shakur's use of lowercase initials suggests that these entities are not natural/essential, but politically determined. Since language inevitably encodes cultural values and particular ways of seeing, for Shakur as for other activists it is understood as simply one more site of struggle. By refusing to submit to the dictates of standard English, Shakur translates her resistance from the social sphere to the world of the text.

In general, the critical rhetoric of the Movement was perceived as much more threatening to the status quo than any particular acts. After all, most political actions can be isolated, neutralized, or otherwise undermined by the state, since how such acts get interpreted and disseminated to a wide audience is determined largely by those who control media. Rhetoric that seeks to organize, raise the consciousness of, and ultimately mobilize *masses* of people, however—particularly across social/economic boundaries—is dangerous. This is the reason Malcolm X and Martin Luther King Jr. had to be permanently silenced, the reason that Fannie Lou Hamer was harassed and tortured, that Fred Hampton was killed, and that several activists from the era, such as Mumia Abu-Jamal (and, until recently, Geronimo Pratt) were imprisoned for their political outspokenness. In *Racial Matters*, Kenneth O'Reilly notes that "physical violence, as opposed to violent rhetoric, was never more than a peripheral part of the black struggle for equality. Political violence, in contrast, was a central part of the FBI response to that struggle—something located within the mainstream of government policy toward blacks" (O'Reilly, 324). Partly because of the intense repression such rhetoric was bringing to bear on the Party, Huey Newton eventually advocated toning down the confrontational language of revolution. This ultimately became one of the underlying factors precipitating the Newton-Cleaver split. Newton felt that a change in the Party's approach was necessary to avoid alienating the masses of Black people. Newton's plan for the Party was to radicalize the people gradually, by first meeting their most basic material needs (food, clothing, and basic health care) and then supplying them with an analysis of group oppression. Cleaver, on the other hand, saw these steps as reformist rather than revolutionary and rejected them in favor of a more militant agenda.

The power of language as a tool for activists is further evidenced not only by the practice of incarcerating political dissidents, but by their treatment once detained. As Davis's and Shakur's personal experiences corroborate, political prisoners are almost always isolated from the general population. They are kept out of circulation not because of any threat they might pose to the physical safety of other prisoners (or vice versa), but because of their facility with words and their ability to act as teachers. Shakur writes that the women in the general population at the Middlesex County Jail laughed when she confided in them that the guards had told her that her life would be endangered in their midst. She remembers: "Gradually, i began to know the women. They were all very kind to me and treated me like a sister. They laughed like hell when i told them that i was supposedly being protected from them" (*Assata*, 53). The attempt to play Shakur and the women against each other is foiled by Shakur's effort to establish community with the women based on her understanding of their common interests under oppression. Angela Davis recalls a similar situation during her time in the Women's House of Detention. She writes: "Originally the jailers had insisted that I had been placed in solitary confinement for my own protection—the women on the corridor would be hostile toward me, they said, because of my Communist politics" (Autobiography, 61). Davis soon discovers, however, that the women are not only supportive and embracing, but eager to learn more about communism and the Movement. Davis subsequently turns their shared confinement into a classroom where such issues as racism, imperialism, and class oppression are enthusiastically discussed (62–63). For Davis and Shakur, the autobiographical project becomes, in part, a subversive way of continuing this pedagogical work (on a larger scale), curtailed during their confinement. Of course, the power of language to alter ways of seeing and understanding extends beyond the bounds of activists' texts; that is, we not only are given a glimpse of how their words influenced others at the time, but also are ultimately pushed to challenge our own ways of knowing in interacting with their stories.

Aside from the women's conscientious attention to the role of language in fostering critical literacy and their recuperation of pivotal events in the story of the Movement, there is yet a third dimension to their autobiographies as political intervention. This third dimension concerns activists' more personal interests and objectives in electing to write their autobiographies. While Davis's and Shakur's recounting of their trials, for example, serves to highlight broad political issues at stake in the larger Black liberation struggle, this recounting also functions in the interests of self-vindication—that is, as a chance to present their own side of the story. Autobiography is an opportunity for activists, no less than other high-profile writers, to reclaim and reconstruct their public images in a manner that is more consistent with their own perceptions of self.

All autobiographers, to varying degrees, engage in self re-creation. Georges Gusdorf once noted that autobiography is less a study of the individual as she is or was than "as [s]he believes and wishes [her]self to be and to have been" (Gusdorf, 45). Even without intending to embellish the past as s/he remembers it, the limitations of memory alone make for an inevitable tension between fact and fiction in autobiographical writing. As Mark Freeman points out in *Rewriting the Self: History, Memory, Narrative*, narrative is created the very moment we seek to impose order and coherence on past experience, particularly when the objective is to explain this past in terms of the present. This ordering typically produces a narrative of cause-and-effect relationships that necessarily delimit the multiple possibilities that might have followed from any single event.

While autobiography as genre thus treads precariously between fact and fiction, what ultimately distinguishes it from fiction is what Philippe Lejeune has referred to as its "referential pact." Lejeune explains that all autobiographical writing involves a referential pact that offers, either explicitly or implicitly, a "definition of the field of the real that is involved and a statement of the modes and the degree of resemblance to which the text lays claim." Unlike fiction, referential texts "claim to provide information about a 'reality' exterior to the text, and so to submit to a test of *verification*" (Lejeune, 22). The pact is perhaps more an issue of ethical intent than of actual outcome, since as Lejeune acknowledges, any act of reconstructing the past necessarily relies upon the subjective and selective nature of memory. Representation is thus not limited to telling *the* truth, but the truth as it appears to the individual, with "allowances for lapses of memory, errors, involuntary distortions, etc." (22). The terms of the referential pact ultimately constitute the grounds on which authorial credibility is judged in autobiographical writing.

While it should be clear that autobiography has fictive components, it is important to note that not all that is fictive (or imaginative) about autobiographical writing is necessarily untrue. To this end, questions raised by Mark Freeman are provocative. If "the making of sense and meaning is indeed part and parcel of both historical understanding and of interpretation more generally," he asks, ". . . can one abide by this demand for the fictive imagination without slipping into the creation of wholesale fictions? More to the point still, how does one begin to distinguish between what might be called 'true fictions' and false ones?" (Freeman, 112). In her essay, "The Site of Memory," Toni Morrison speaks to precisely this issue by posing a distinction between fact and truth, noting that what may not be factual (i.e., not specifically documented in the historical record) may nevertheless be true. She further asserts that the "critical distinction for [her] is not the difference between fact and fiction, but the distinction between fact and truth" (Morrison, 113). Referring specifically to African American emancipation narratives and the silences surrounding the individual authors' interior lives (a convention of the genre as opposed to an indication that they lacked interior lives), Morrison notes that while it is impossible to fill such silences with facts from the historical record explaining what the writers thought, felt, and believed, it *is* possible to explore those silences imaginatively by focusing on the truth of their condition. As if carrying Morrison's sentiment to its logical conclusion, Freeman argues pointedly for reconceptualizing what is understood as *truth* in autobiographical practice. He asks: "Can we not say, in fact, that the reality of living in time requires narrative reflection and that narrative reflection, in turn, opens the way toward a more comprehensive and expansive conception of truth itself?" (Freeman, 32). Because activists' narratives seek to make vital corrections to the historical record, the issues of memory and truth in autobiographical practice would seem to have important implications for how we receive and evaluate their stories. This is true not only with respect to how the narratives challenge dominant ways of knowing that are institutionally reinforced in our culture, but also with respect to how the writers reconstruct their own images and modes of being during the period recounted.

For Davis and Shakur, writing autobiography affords the opportunity to counter the barrage of negative press (and often misinformation) that played a prominent role in both of their high-profile cases. Resisting the tyranny of the sound bite that would silence the complex issues involved in each of their cases, they offer their own words to supply crucial but institutionally elided details. Their narratives endeavor to reinscribe the contexts that help others to make sense of their particular predicaments and to better appreciate their motivation for involvement in radical resistance struggle. Partly because of her differing sensibility and partly because her narrative appears so many years after her involvement with the Black Panther Party, the kind of self-recovery evident in Brown's autobiography has a distinctly different flavor. More so than with either Davis or Shakur, Brown's gaze is an internal one. In many ways, Brown's *Taste of Power* reveals a conscientious effort to minimize psychic dissonance between her own past and present states of political consciousness. Given the responses of others in the Movement who seem to remember her quite differently from the way she remembers herself, Brown's recreating of self is largely about reconciling and laying to rest still troubling ghosts from her past. Although Brown, for example, frequently portrays herself in the autobiography as demonstrating a proto-feminist sensibility vis-à-vis other women in the Party (e.g., her membership in the "clique" [A *Taste*, 192] or her visible resentment upon being asked to cook for and/or serve food to men during Party gatherings), the perceptions of her held by women outside the Party suggest a different story. Brown admits that she was accused by some feminists of being a "lackey for men" (367). At one point, she ruminates over her passion for songwriting and realizes that even in that she had sought the attention and favor of men (310). In A *Taste*, Brown endeavors to fashion (by virtue of what she chooses to include and to omit from the narrative) a past identity less at odds with her present consciousness.

In A *Taste of Power*, the referential pact (along with its parameters) is explicitly stated. While Brown is engaged, in part, in telling the story of the Party, she is emphatic that A *Taste* be understood as an avowedly subjective account of the period. Her disclaimer appears to distance the autobiography from the kinds of expectations normally associated with purely historical (or even other activists') writing about the period. In the introduction, her use first of the indefinite article and then alternately of the first person and possessive pronouns is instructive. She begins: "This is *a* chronicle of the life of a black woman-chile in America. It is *my* life. Reflected here is a life *as I* lived it, my thoughts and feelings *as I* remember them" (xi; emphasis added). In subsequently proclaiming her intent to be "faithful to both fact and feeling" throughout, she satisfies the terms of Lejeune's referential pact of autobiographical writing. Brown introduces *A Taste* as a chronicle of her experiences as *she* remembers them. Although the text travels back to her childhood years growing up in the projects of North Philadelphia, Brown's primary focus is on the time she spent as a politically active member of the Black Panther Party. This is further indicated by the way the narrative is framed; it begins with an announcement of her rise to power within the organization and closes with her flight from the same. Presumably, Brown's attention to her early years is intended to shed light on her later activities. In any event, the referential pact seems to be most relevant to the story Brown remembers about her life with the Panthers.

As if anticipating the kind of criticisms that emerged following the book's publication, Brown opens *A Taste* with a statement about autobiographical practice and accountability. In the effort to re-present her personal exchanges with others during the period (a point on which she has been broadly criticized), Brown explains that she "relied on [her] knowledge of opinions held, and [her] recollection of articulated ideas and very specific words in their context" (xi). Several lengthy quotes, as more than one reviewer of the book noted, inevitably raise questions of authenticity. Among the more egregious and frequently cited examples is a remarkably detailed monologue in which Brown attempts to give voice to the breadth of Huey Newton's political vision. For approximately four pages Brown quotes Newton expounding upon his theory of "intercommunalism" (277–81). Newton's monologue describes the demise of nationhood under late capitalism and its replacement by a "collection of integrated communities" subject to the interests of a hegemonic power. On the issue of Newton's monologue alone, both Jill Nelson and Michelle Wallace, in separate reviews for the *Washington Post* (Nelson, B2) and the *New York Times Book Review* (Wallace, 7) respectively, raised questions about Brown's credibility. Wallace, for instance, noted that while *A Taste* is "chilling, well written and profoundly entertaining," it is not "distinguished for its honesty." Nelson even used the word "unconscionable" to describe Brown's extensive quoting. Nelson's word choice is particularly noteworthy because it suggests an ethical breach of the implied referential contract in autobiographical writing.

Clearly, the liberty Brown takes with quoting creates contrary impulses for her readers: she asks that they temporarily suspend disbelief, even though this is an expectation normally reserved for fiction. This dilemma of how to render past conversations is perhaps more effectively resolved in David Hilliard's 1993 autobiography, *This Side of Glory*. Unlike Brown, Hilliard often cites other texts (usually statements published during the period in different formats) when reproducing lengthy quotes. In other instances, he adopts a documentary style, incorporating individuals' retrospective accounts from interviews conducted specifically for the autobiography. In this way, his rewriting of history is more avowedly collaborative than either Brown's, Davis's, or Shakur's. (Of course, Hilliard's narrative is also collaborative in that it is written with Lewis Cole.)

Although any attempt in autobiography to directly quote past exchanges raises issues of credibility, some degree of transgression is readily overlooked by readers and critics for the sake of narrative flow and interest (the kinds of qualities, incidentally, for which Wallace praises Brown's book). Brown herself seems acutely aware of the limitations of memory in reconstructing the past. She in fact acknowledges in her own introduction the ways in which memory is precarious (comparing it poetically to a "fragile spirit"), and also the way in which it tends to be complicated by the imaginative process. Memory, she writes, "may be a river of reality that gathers dreams and desires and change in its flow." Such an approach reflects what Arnold Krupat has described as the "conversation between historia and poesis, documentation and creation" that is always taking place in autobiography (Krupat, 161). While it is scarcely worth debating the likelihood of anyone being able to recall verbatim a conversation that took place more than twenty years previously, Brown's extensive quoting of Newton, for example, is pedagogically strategic, since it serves to disseminate Newton's political ideas. The liberties Brown takes in re-presenting the past, particularly as it pertains to the extended quotes attributed to Newton and others, are ultimately less interesting (in the context of discussing political autobiography) as a debate over fact vs. fiction than—as Toni Morrison reminds us—as a debate over fact vs. truth. While there is ample cause to question the *fact* of such an exchange (i.e., the manner in which it occurred, the precise words that were used, or the exact setting in which the exchange took place), the *truth* of the incident is not untenable.

Following the implications of Morrison's claim that historical fact reveals little about the truth of experience, A Taste illustrates that that part of autobiography which tends toward the imaginative (or the not factual) may nevertheless be valuable as truth.

It is likely that Brown, like David Hilliard, relied in several instances on research to bolster her own memories. A reference to Newton's *Revolutionary Suicide* (1973), for instance, is listed in the continuation of the copyright page (451). Another 1973 text coauthored by Newton, *In Search of Common Ground: Conversations with Erik Erikson and Huey P. Newton*, is likewise cited (282). Just as much of Newton's theorizing (that appears in A Taste) on intercommunalism, the rise of the "global village," and Black Americans as the revolutionary vanguard can be found in *In Search of Common Ground* (29–32), much of the content of an exchange recorded in A Taste between Newton, Hilliard, and Brown as the three strategized over breakfast in a New York hotel room (248) can be traced to passages from Newton's 1972 collection of essays, *To Die for the People*. In the latter case, Brown quotes Newton explaining the significance of the Party's "Survival Programs" as well as the role of violence/the gun in the revolution (consistent with the teachings of Mao Zedong). With only a few syntactical alterations, the same content appears in *To Die for the People* as part of the chapter "On the Defection of Eldridge Cleaver from the Black Panther Party and the Defection of the Black Panther Party from the Black Community: April 17, 1971." Like other activists' narratives, Brown's autobiography reveals an intertextual sharing of information and ideas, with the latter treated as communal property within the Movement.

Brown's inclusion of lengthy quotes, however, is only one issue on which her credibility as autobiographer has been challenged. In "Sister Act: Symbol and Substance in Black Women's Leadership," a scathing review ostensibly comparing A Taste to recent life stories by/about two other Black women activists, former Panther Kathleen Cleaver charges Brown with both a "reckless disregard for truth" and a glaring lack of self-reflexivity (K. Cleaver, 97). Cleaver's review is an "ostensible comparison" because A Taste is clearly the focus of the exercise; neither Kay Mill's biography of Fannie Lou Hamer, *This Little Light of Mine*, nor Charlayne Hunter-Gault's autobiography, *In My Place*, is held by Cleaver to the same rigorous criteria that Brown's text is. Perhaps because of

Brown's mostly unflattering depiction of Eldridge and Kathleen Cleaver in *A Taste* (Cleaver never addresses this directly), the unusually caustic words Cleaver chooses to describe Brown's text betray a subtext of antagonism. Her choice of adjectives to contrast Brown's narrative with the other two are illustrative: Hunter-Gault's autobiography is generally praised as "moving," "funny," "lyrical," and even "endearing" (92), while Brown's is dismissed as often malicious, "careless," "flawed," and "incoherent" (97–98). Although Cleaver's motives as critic may be suspect given the history of antagonism between herself and Brown, many of her claims concerning Brown's tendency toward historical revisionism are supported by other sources.

In "Sister Act," Cleaver hones in on Brown's apparent carelessness with dates, her tendency toward revisionism in terms of her own beliefs and actions at the time, inaccuracies concerning Party history and policy, and the improbable attribution of certain statements and dialogue to particular Party members (97).[2] Cleaver declares: "Despite an apparently sensational subject matter, recounted in the style of a fast-paced novel, Brown's narrative suffers from a certain myopia. Because she rarely connects the events of her own life with what is going on in the larger world, and infrequently supplies dates to the incidents she describes, her story has a pervasive sense of unreality" (95). Cleaver joins reviewer Jill Nelson in noting instances in the book where Brown's chronology is troubling. Frequently, for example, Brown recalls past time by events rather than by dates. In one such example, she mentions at the beginning of chapter 10 that it had been a year since Bobby Hutton's ("the first to fall in struggle") murder. Readers wanting the exact year either have to recall the date of Hutton's murder or flip backward through the text. Brown's way of telling time, however, is characteristic of the oral tradition in which recollection/memory is sustained associatively rather than through the recounting of dates. That is, Hutton's death is a more

---

[2] Interestingly, in her effort to undermine Brown's text, Cleaver makes a few factual errors of her own. She claims, for instance, that Brown erroneously attributes the origin of the Black Panther *name* (i.e., the BPP for Self-Defense) to the Deacons for Defense. What Brown actually writes, however, is that the Panthers modeled their own organization after the *spirit* of the Deacons for Defense. Though Cleaver misses the fact, she and Brown agree that the Panther *logo* originated with the Lowndes County (Alabama) Freedom Organization.

important marker of time than the numerical year (1968) in which it happened. Shakur's text is similar to Brown's in this respect; dates are rarely mentioned. Brown's way of recalling the past is thus the creating of a counter-history that may be easier to remember.

Beyond a sloppiness with dates, Cleaver also accuses Brown of anachronism and historical revisionism. As an example of the former, she points out that Brown claims to have bought and read *Soul on Ice* in late 1967 (*A Taste*, 121) when the book was not published until February 1968 (K. Cleaver, 97). As yet another example, Cleaver refers to Brown's depiction of Bunchy Carter using the phrase "to die for the people" when it allegedly did not become part of Party parlance until *after* Carter's death. As an instance of historical revisionism, Cleaver cites Brown's apparent change in attitude toward David Hilliard, whose leadership she allegedly was very critical of during the period.

More than Cleaver's charges concerning Brown's slippage with dates, the charges of historical revisionism point to ways Brown appears to use the autobiography to advance a personal as well as political agenda. Cleaver saliently argues that Brown fails to provide important information about the context of her own rise to power. She notes, for instance, that by 1974 the "internal dissension, external repression, and the exhaustion of that underlying momentum that had generated the mass movements for social change for the past twenty years had left the party decimated. It had shrunk from a national organization with over fifty chapters into a small body with only a few branch offices outside of Oakland" (K. Cleaver, 90).[3] Cleaver's claim is corroborated by Hugh Pearson, author of *The Shadow of the Panther*, who indicates that by the time Brown moved from Los Angeles to Oakland to assume the post of Minister of Information (formerly held by Eldridge Cleaver), Newton had already closed most of the national branches and summoned all remaining Party members to the west coast. Pearson further notes that "by the beginning of 1972, the party was down to approximately 150 core members engaged in various pursuits" (Pearson, 247). By then, the

---

[3] Contrary to Cleaver, William Van DeBurg maintains that, at its height (circa 1970), the Black Panther Party had offices in 35 cities in 19 states plus Washington, D.C. Van DeBurg adds that the Party had also established international chapters in England, France, and Israel (Van DeBurg, 155).

New York Panther 21 and other sympathizers with the Eldridge Cleaver faction (including Shakur) had also split with the national leadership. In *Inadmissible Evidence*, Evelyn Williams declares that she "knew of no active branch of the Black Panther Party after its COINTELPRO-engineered demise in 1971" (Williams, 195). (Williams's statement implicitly acknowledges the New York Cleaver faction as the only legitimate continuation of the Party's original agenda.) Descriptions in Shakur's narrative of the climate in the Party created by FBI infiltration, rampant paranoia among Panther members, and Newton's expulsions of activists also tend to support Williams's and Cleaver's claims. Shakur recalls that by the early 1970s, "the easy, friendly openness had been replaced by fear and paranoia. The beautiful revolutionary creativity i had loved so much was gone. And replaced by dogmatic stagnation" (*Assata*, 231). As a consequence of fierce internal dissension leading up to and following the ideological split between the Newton and Cleaver factions of the Party, many Panthers were either expelled or voluntarily left the organization. Some, like Shakur, no longer considered the Black Panther Party to be a revolutionary force, and chose to rechannel their energies into the Black Liberation Army, a group launched by Cleaver loyalists (Pearson, 272).

Like Emily Dickinson's enigmatic line, "tell the truth but tell it slant," *A Taste* ultimately does just that. The tension that emerges between truth and fact in Brown's narrative is less the result of "lapses of memory, errors, involuntary distortions"—all of which are accounted for in Lejeune's referential pact—than of Brown's will toward self-vindication. The comments of others—perhaps Kathleen Cleaver most vocally—suggest that Brown deliberately manipulates truth in *A Taste* to refashion her own image in a more flattering light. When *A Taste* is read alongside other sources, Brown's memory appears notably selective with regard to at least two consequential episodes: the mysterious disappearance of Betty Van Patter (hired by Brown to maintain the Party's financial books), and a fatal shootout between the Panthers and Ron Karenga's US Organization in 1968 on the campus of UCLA. Brown's recollection of both incidents is important because what she chooses to reveal and to withhold says potentially different things about her character.

In his book *The Shadow of the Panther*, Hugh Pearson writes that Betty

Van Patter, a White woman recommended to Brown as an adept accoun-
tant by a then mutual friend, David Horowitz, accepted a job with the
Party in the early 1970s. Van Patter, however, soon fell into Brown's
disfavor for asking too many questions about some of the Party's dubious
expenditures. Van Patter's later mysterious disappearance raised suspi-
cions about the Party's probable involvement. When questioned on the
matter, Brown allegedly reacted defensively and even sought to vigorously discourage further probing into the issue by sympathetic Party
members (Pearson, 272). David Horowitz, in particular, claims to have
been indirectly threatened by Brown when he continued to inquire into
Van Patter's disappearance (Pearson, 272). Horowitz, a former editor at
Ramparts magazine turned fan of Huey Newton, took an active interest
in the Panther school and was a devoted supporter of the Party until he
became disenchanted with Brown's handling of the Van Patter affair,
among other troubling incidents in the later years of the Party. Although no material evidence has ever been produced to link Brown directly to the murder, Pearson's sources suggest that Brown may have
conferred with Newton (who at the time was in exile in Cuba) over the
situation and been given either the order or the approval for Van Patter's
murder (Pearson, 272).

Although Brown disavows any knowledge of the circumstances surrounding Van Patter's disappearance, she does concede in A *Taste* that
Van Patter's perpetual inquisitiveness *was* annoying. Brown writes: "Immediately Betty began asking Norma, and every other Panther with
whom she had contact, about the sources of our cash, or the exact nature
of this or that expenditure. Her job was to order and balance our books
and records, not to investigate them. I ordered her to cease her interro-
gations. She continued. I knew that I had made a mistake in hiring her"
(A *Taste*, 364). Brown appears defensive in the autobiography when she
seeks to reframe the incident by raising questions about Van Patter's
character and past. While Brown refers more than once to Van Patter's
having a prison record, for instance, Pearson maintains that "there is no
evidence that Van Patter ever had a criminal record" (Pearson, 272).

Reiterating a sentiment expressed in Cleaver's critique, Michelle Wallace proposes that Brown "is a little too precise in the descriptions of
crimes that fail again and again to implicate her" (Wallace, 7). Jill Nelson similarly observes that "Brown has an uncanny ability to be off the

scene when prosecutable events occur" (Nelson, B2). A case in point is Brown's rendering of the shootout between the Panthers and the US Organization on the campus of UCLA—a second critical incident in which Brown's version of the story is at odds with what others remember. The violence erupted on January 17, 1969, following a meeting between the two organizations to discuss the founding of a Black Studies program at UCLA. An official account of the circumstances precipitating the shootout, which left Panthers Alprentice "Bunchy" Carter and John Huggins dead, remains to date ambiguous. In *her* recollection of the incident, Brown writes that after the meeting adjourned, she was manhandled by one of Karenga's "robots" forcefully enough that "the button snapped off [her] black leather coat." Brown's recollection of the verbal exchange that preceded the physical confrontation is peculiarly one-sided, though. She recounts simply being warned by the US member to "watch what you say" (*A Taste*, 164). Brown relays in detail what she *thought* of her assailant: "The only thing that differentiated that Karenga robot from the others, I noted, was the mustache outline he had drawn over his protruding lips with eyeliner. I could hardly feel frightened of anybody wearing a painted-on manhood. Indeed, I had an impulse to smear the thing. I was certainly not terrorized as I tried to move past him" (164). However, her rendering of the confrontation implies that these thoughts were not actually verbalized. Brown indicates that Bunchy Carter, who observed the exchange, first inquired what the US member had said to her, and then encouraged her, in the future, to slap anyone accosting or disrespecting her in a similar manner (165). Brown claims she then left the scene only to be startled moments later by the outburst of gunfire.

Both Kathleen Cleaver and Ron Karenga, in separate accounts, dispute Brown's version of the shootout. In "A Response to Muhammad Ahmad," Karenga charges that Brown's role in "precipitating the incident" has been "played down or covered up" (Karenga, 55). Disappointingly, Karenga neglects to elaborate on what this "role" actually consisted of. Instead, he cites a July 10, 1969, *Los Angeles Sentinel* article to substantiate his claim. The *Sentinel* article, however, does not actually document Brown's *precipitation* of the incident. Rather, the article merely confirms that she was a sought-after witness. The article additionally notes that lawyers prosecuting the murders of Carter and Huggins had to that point been unsuccessful in serving subpoenas on either Albert Armour or Elaine Brown, both named (among two others) as witnesses ("Murder Trial Maneuvering," A-11). In *Racial Matters*, Kenneth O'Reilly indicates that Brown was eventually called to testify for the state at the murder trial (O'Reilly, 306). George and Larry Stiner, two of five members of Karenga's Simba Wachuka charged in the shooting deaths, received life sentences.

Cleaver, who similarly neglected to go into detail, disputed Brown's version of the UCLA incident during a public lecture at Cornell University on April 19, 1994. Both Cleaver and Karenga strongly imply that there was considerably more to Brown's encounter with the US member than *A Taste* reveals. By their accounts, the shootout ensued after Carter intervened *on Brown's behalf* (a move prompted by both a reactionary chivalry and the imperative to defend Brown as a representative of the Party). By the way the episode is portrayed in *A Taste*, however, probable cause for the assault by the US member (the FBI-manipulated rivalry between the Panthers and US notwithstanding) is difficult to infer. Although admittedly present just moments before the eruption of gunfire, Brown seems to have no insight into the events that transpired. To confuse matters further, Brown contradicted her own account in the autobiography, in an interview shortly after Pantheon released *A Taste*, by claiming that she in fact *saw* who shot Carter. She states there that "the Pathfinders [sic—Pantheon?] lawyers made me take the name out, but it's in the drafts" (Sinclair, "A Conversation," 24). Did she, as Cleaver and Karenga insinuate, deliberately instigate a confrontation (requiring rescue) in a setting already rife with tension? After all, Brown's rescue by powerful men is a motif throughout the autobiography. While it certainly would be absurd to hold Brown *responsible* for any so-called "chivalric" responses of Party men (here, the blame is more appropriately laid at the foot of sexism), any deliberate manipulation of such responses would necessarily be problematic.

More blatantly than Davis's and Shakur's narratives, *A Taste* reveals multiple levels of personal intervention at work. That is, apart from the attempt to recuperate her own public image in the wake of negative press or to defend individual and group actions undertaken to advance the struggle (features common to all three women's narratives), Brown's autobiography as personal intervention also seeks to refashion a past

"I" that appears less at odds with her present consciousness. While the women's narratives as political intervention challenge hegemonic history and dominant ways of knowing, their texts as personal intervention reveal, to differing degrees, self-recreation as an integral aspect of the autobiographical project. Brown's particular motives for recreating her own image vis-à-vis select episodes in A *Taste* aside, the disparity between what she remembers or chooses to tell about her own life and what others seem to remember about her raises interesting questions about whether activists' use of autobiography as *personal* intervention is at odds with the objectives of their texts as *political* intervention. Put another way: if authorial credibility is in question with regard to some matters, doesn't this affect how we process a writer's testimony about other matters? In what ways is Brown's recreating of self tied to substantive political consequences? Activists' texts repeatedly reveal that there is little separation between the two realms: i.e., what is personal is almost always political and vice versa. The effectiveness of Davis's, Shakur's, and Brown's narratives as political intervention relies in part on their skill as storytellers: their ability to map the personal onto the larger political terrain in provocative and engaging ways. Sometimes their stories create new myths even as they set out to challenge old ones. Occasionally their stories alter facts, but usually with an eye toward conveying some larger truth. Individually, their stories are less *the* truth than *a* truth about the Movement and its principal players, which acquires its larger meaning only in relation to the other stories also being told. Individual activists' recollections are constantly challenged intertextually by the reflections of others on the same period. Reading Brown's narrative against others from and about the period underscores the precarious nature of memory in autobiographical practice, and at the same time complicates (in useful ways) any simplistic notion of truth. Ultimately, one of the most compelling aspects of activists' autobiographies may be the attention they inevitably call to the politics of how history and truth are constructed.

Chapter 5

Gender and Power Dynamics in 1960s Black Nationalist Struggle

In Pratibha Parmar's 1992 film, *A Place of Rage*, African American poet, essayist, and activist June Jordan shares her recollection of the ways the spirit of nationalism that was so pervasive during the Black Power Movement informed practices and modes of thought that were sometimes quite repressive. She recalls, for example, conversations in which Black women, eager to show support for Black men, actually debated the appropriate distance they ought to walk behind their men. Jordan also recalls, on other occasions, the racist assumptions implicit in Black activists' dubious attempts to define an essential or authentic Black identity. The fact that most activists failed to meet whatever criteria were ultimately established underscored, for Jordan, the absurdity in such thinking. Davis, Shakur, and Brown, in their attention to gender and racial dynamics during the Movement, speak to these kinds of contradictions, while also providing important information about the sometimes radically different experiences of men and women in resistance struggle. In the context of the larger struggle for individual and group self-determination, such differences include how women experienced intimate relationships, how they approached parenthood, and how they negotiated interaction with the dominant culture.

At the same time that the women critique racially and sexually repressive practices within the dominant culture, they point out how many of the same dynamics continued to manifest themselves inside the liberation movement. Much of their critique addresses the quality of male-female interpersonal relationships. In "On the Issue of Roles," writer and activist Toni Cade Bambara suggests that the first prerequisite to revolution involves each individual completing an inventory of self. Defining the individual as the most fundamental revolutionary unit, she goes on to argue that individuals, therefore, "must be purged of poison and lies that assault the ego and threaten the heart, that hazard the next larger unit—the couple or pair, that jeopardize the still larger unit—the family or cell, that put the entire movement in peril" (Bambara, 109). In the spirit of Bambara's words, the women's narratives studied here repeatedly insist upon this link between the personal and the political. This way of knowing, which begins with a critique of one's own ways of being, is significant because it points to a relational rather than a dyadic model of power, with important implications for how activists wage revolutionary struggle. If power is, as Michel Foucault argues, "always already there . . . [and] one is never 'outside' it . . . there are [consequently] no 'margins' for those who break with the system to gambol in" (Foucault, *Power/Knowledge*, 141–42). When power is understood less as a thing that exists somewhere outside of individuals, and more as a matrix of relations people continually negotiate, then time and energy devoted to self-critique and reflection must be regarded as anything but frivolous.

Effectively challenging or dismantling structures of domination first requires an awareness of how one participates in them, that is, how one's individual actions and values function either to maintain or to disrupt dominant forms. In the end, the struggle outside will always be compromised if one's "own house," as Bambara concludes, is not in order. Of course, this is no simple matter. There is the very real question of whether individuals *can* get their houses in order while living under the particular psychological and material consequences of oppression. Cognizant of this dilemma, what Bambara and other women activists propose is the need to revision liberation struggle as work that must be waged on multiple levels and fronts simultaneously. In her powerful conclusion to "On the Issue of Roles," Bambara cautions:

> Not all speed is movement. Running off to mimeograph a fuck-whitey leaflet, leaving your mate to brood is not revolutionary. Hopping a plane to rap to someone else's "community" while your son struggles alone with the Junior Scholastic assignment on "The Dark Continent" is not revolutionary. Sitting around mouthing incorrect niggers while your father goes upside your mother's head is not revolutionary. . . . If your house is not in order, you ain't in order. It is so much easier to be out there than right here. The revolution ain't out there. Yet. But it is here. Should be. And

arguing that instant-coffee-ten-minutes-to-midnight alibi to justify hasty-headed dealings with your mate is shit. Ain't no such animal as an instant guerrilla. (Bambara, 110)

It is worth quoting Bambara at length because what she expresses strikes at the heart of the particular dilemma Black revolutionaries faced during the era—that is, the dilemma of how to relate to each other and to the Black community while laboring to identify and abolish their own complicity in repressive values and gender role expectations associated with American capitalist bourgeois culture. In their essay "Is the Black Male Castrated?" authors Jean Carey Bond and Patricia Peery cite, as a serious shortcoming of the Movement, the inability of activists to redefine masculinity and femininity in terms other than those set forth by the dominant culture. Because those characteristics traditionally associated with masculinity in this culture (e.g., ruggedness, aggressiveness, bravery, and emotional and physical strength) are necessarily demanded of women involved in revolutionary struggle, Black women in 1960s radical struggle found themselves in a peculiar situation. In transcending traditional feminine roles and gender expectations in order to participate actively in the struggle, they sometimes encountered rejection from their Black male counterparts precisely because they were no longer seen as feminine. Brown, for instance, writes: "In general, Black Panther women were stripped of the pretty things, the 'bourgeois' sweetness that could have made them glamorous women, the kind that I saw Huey adored, despite his revolutionized ways. Panther women were hard, in a way—soldiers, comrades, not pretty little things" (A Taste, 260).

In a single paragraph devoted to both her marriage and its dissolution, Shakur suggests that her union with Louis Chesimard (while both were student activists at CCNY) dissolved after just one year primarily because they were unable to renegotiate traditional gender-role expectations (Assata, 196). The failure to readjust gender-role expectations to reflect more appropriately the particular circumstances in which activists found themselves also contributed to the devastating perpetuation of racist and sexist assumptions associated with the coextensive myths of Black matriarchy and Black male emasculation. Both myths were popularized largely by Senator Daniel Patrick Moynihan's now infamous March 1965 report, The Negro Family: The Case for National Action. Bond and Peery argue that "It is the transference of values, which work for the oppressor in the capitalist context, to the milieu of the oppressed, where they are dysfunctional, that has pitted Black man against Black woman and vice versa—a situation which, needless to say, is anathema to the pursuit of self-determination" (Bond and Peery, 117). Adherence to values that perpetuate the patriarchal order (resulting in, among other things, the objectification of women's bodies and the devaluation of women's work) hurt African Americans as a group by undermining the solidarity needed to mount unified (i.e., across gender) resistance to shared racial oppression.

While the Party's rejection in principle of the commoditization of intimate relationships under capitalism (specifically, the ownership of one's lover/partner) was liberating in many ways, the freedom to be intimate with multiple partners predictably translated into different consequences for women than for men. The combination of biology (the possibility of pregnancy) and ideology (the Party's rejection of birth control as genocide) created a situation in which women inevitably had more to lose. As the narratives by Brown, Shakur, and Davis repeatedly attest, men often managed to maintain male privilege even as radical shifts appeared to take place in the nature of interpersonal relations. While Newton, in accordance with Party ideology, rejected possessiveness in the context of intimate relationships, Brown notes that he often made it very clear to her potential suitors that she was, in fact, his woman (*A Taste*, 246). That is, his woman *along with* the many other women whose company he also continued to enjoy. Significantly, Brown—because of the power differential between herself and Newton specifically, and between women and men in general—could make no similar claim (i.e., one that was bound to be respected) on Newton. Although Bobby Seale maintains in his autobiography, *A Lonely Rage*, that "[t]he principle that backed up love relationships among Party members was simply that those who did not have an established one-to-one relationship with someone had the right, male or female, to make love with whomever they desired" (Seale, *Rage*, 187), which party in the relationship enjoyed the privilege of defining whether or not the relationship was an "established one-to-one" was another matter. The narratives repeatedly suggest that men were often the ones who assumed this prerogative. David Hilliard's extramarital involvement with Brenda

Presley, described in *This Side of Glory*, is exemplary, as it violated (by Hilliard's own admission) the one-to-one relationship that Pat, his wife, assumed she and Hilliard shared.

Repeatedly, Brown suggests the many ways in which sexual politics were manipulated within the Movement to reinscribe patriarchal privilege. Newton, Hilliard, and Seale, in their respective autobiographies, likewise attest to the frequency with which men conflated women's capitulation to demands for sex with their commitment to the revolution. Brown recalls pressure from Earl Anthony, who reminded her, for instance, that "a true Sister would be happy to sleep with a revolutionary Brother" (*A Taste*, 115). That women were additionally charged with the task of producing offspring for the revolution complicated matters further. The charge rendered the practice of abortion particularly shameful. Brown's guilt in the aftermath of an abortion she elected to have toward the end of her affiliation with the Party is most likely tied to the residual influence of Party ideology condemning the use of contraceptives. She writes: "The immorality of it stung something deep in me. It was not in thinking that I had killed someone. I had done something worse. I had prevented someone from coming into being" (434). Shakur writes that when she discovered she was pregnant, she refused to consider abortion for precisely this reason.

Encouraged to regard birth control as genocide, many women who surrendered reproductive control of their bodies to the Party's line were left to rear on their own children born of tenuous relationships. Men, on the other hand, generally retained the freedom to accept or renege on parental responsibilities. Brown, who carried to term her pregnancy by Masai Hewit, for instance, was left to rear their daughter, Ericka, without Hewit's support. Brown writes that in fact she learned during her fourth month of pregnancy that Hewit had married another woman (*A Taste*, 199). When Brown confided her feelings over the matter to David Hilliard, Hilliard chastised her for being petty, for allowing the " 'subjective' to supersede the 'objective' " (199). The implication is not only that mind and body can be separated/severed (an assumption peculiar to Western rational thought), but also that interpersonal relationships are somehow outside the realm of politics. Both of these assumptions are repeatedly challenged by women's experiences.

The fact that the Party put no real provisions in place to support its position on birth control resulted in a serious contradiction between ideology and practice. As Bambara once pointed out in "The Pill: Genocide or Liberation?" to simply bring children into the world is not enough. More than simply warm bodies, the revolution, Bambara argued, is in need of "super-people" who can think in ways that will effectively advance the struggle (Bambara, 168). Significantly, raising "super-people" requires a commitment of time, energy, and resources. In order to nurture children who will grow up strong and healthy, women themselves must first be at a point in their own lives where they are intellectually, physically, and spiritually fortified. Accordingly, access to birth control is important because it allows women to choose when (or if) they can best meet this challenge. As feminists have long argued, the loss of reproductive freedom represents for women a loss of self-determination. Of course, any threat to women's self-determination, as the texts by Davis, Brown, and Shakur repeatedly insist, necessarily undermines the liberation struggle as a whole.

Both Brown's and Shakur's texts address the politics of motherhood for women activists, challenging, in the process, many traditional expectations. In Brown's text there is tension between what she appears to recognize as the larger society's expectations for her as a mother and the demands associated with her own work as a radical activist. Acknowledging guilt over her inability to function in both roles simultaneously, she laments being unable to lavish on her daughter the kind of attention society proposes any "good" mother should be able to give. Referring to Ericka, she writes: "I wanted somebody to tell her it was all right if I never baked a cake, all right if I knew nothing about teething, or what she was supposed to be eating at this stage. I wanted somebody to make amends for what I would not do for her, because I was doing this intangible thing, with this grand idea about my role in it. I wanted to explain myself" (A Taste, 250). With the exception of one detailed reunion she describes with Ericka after an extended absence (249–51), there is almost no sustained discussion of the impact—either on her or on her daughter—of their continued separation. Brown's references to her role as mother are few and far between. Although she includes details surrounding Ericka's birth, she says very little afterward about making the adjustment to having a child. Instead, the narrative jumps ahead to three months later to talk about her prospective trip to North Korea to meet with Eldridge Cleaver (in exile) and her preparations to have Ericka stay with her comrades (217–18). Her mention of her daughter in other places in the text seems more obligatory than anything else. This is not to find fault with Brown's approach to mothering. Rather, the point is that her fleeting references to Ericka in the text seem designed largely to appease an imagined audience's expectations for how a "mother" *should* think/behave. That is, such moments may be less credible as accurate portrayals of Brown's own state of mind at the time than as an indication of Brown's present desire to avoid her readers' disapproval. While narrating her sojourn with Cleaver in Beijing, Brown writes simply "I had been gone from my baby for over two months" (231). No further elaboration follows her statement. In thwarting any expectations for additional detail (for example, she does not address her feelings about such a prolonged absence), Brown's silences around motherhood, even though ambivalent, have important implications for feminist theory. Readers who are conscious of their own reactions, for instance, may find cause to evaluate their own values and assumptions about women as mothers.

Even as she expresses some guilt over her inability to be there for Ericka, Brown also indicates that much about traditional motherhood— had she been able to fulfill that role—would have been too personally stifling. While she acknowledges her own mother's tenacity in being there consistently for her as a child in ways that she herself is not there for Ericka, Brown also suggests that her mother's criticism of her is mixed with a sense of envy for Brown's capacity to exercise choices that she either did not or could not as a young adult. After enduring her mother's lecture over her shortcomings as a mother, Brown concludes: "She was right about everything I was not. I just listened. I did not want to be her. *She did not want to be her*" (251; emphasis added). While Brown acknowledges the imperfect quality of her own mothering based on the conventional expectations of motherhood in American culture, she nevertheless avoids romanticizing traditional models which too often result in women's self-denial and alienation. What is missing in Brown's assessment of her own and her mother's approach to motherhood, however, is an alternative model. Given the Party's praise and promotion of motherhood, it is ironic that no real attention was given to this matter as part of an ongoing formulation of revolutionary strategy.

Though Brown mentions her association with other pregnant women in the Party (Ericka Huggins, for example), there is generally silence around the way women labored collectively under the often contradictory expectations and assumptions associated with being both mothers and radical activists. It is clear from both Brown's and Shakur's texts that each was able to rely upon a supportive community of other women to care for their children in their absence. However, what remains unclear is how and to what extent women were able to liberate themselves *psychologically* (as opposed to simply materially) from diametrically opposed cultural expectations. This theoretical silence in women's activist work is worthy of further critical exploration.

Because she was incarcerated at the time of her daughter's birth, Shakur, like Brown, defied conventional expectations for women who are mothers. While still in the womb, Kakuya symbolized, for her mother, hope and promise for a future beyond the suffering, violence, and repression of the present. Shakur concedes that, prior to her discussions with Kamau (Kakuya's father) during their joint trial, she had never wanted children because of the hostile circumstances into which they would necessarily be born. Reflecting on the condition of the ancestors, however, she ultimately determined that to deny her own desire for a child would be, in the end, to grant her oppressors too much power. She reasons: "[I]'m not letting these parasites, these oppressors, these greedy racist swine make me kill my children in my mind, before they are even born" (*Assata*, 93). Having a child thus becomes for Shakur another act of resistance. The unborn child ensures that the circle is unbroken. Shakur's poem, "Love," addressing the growing life in her womb, is illustrative. She writes:

> *Love is contraband in Hell,*
> *cause love is an acid*
> *that eats away bars.*
> *But you, me, and tomorrow*
> *hold hands and make vows*
> *that struggle will multiply.*
> *The hacksaw has two blades.*
> *The shotgun has two barrels.*
> *We are pregnant with freedom.*
> *We are a conspiracy. (130)*

The power and resilience of the resistance struggle multiplies through the birth of her child. For Shakur, there is continuity between the fallen, the living, and the yet unborn. Each draws sustenance and purpose from that which came before. The "we" in the poem is resonant, and seems to encompass not just Shakur and her unborn child, but all those who make up the struggle for freedom. Following the African tradition, the child belongs less to individuals than to an entire community. This is a significant point since birth mothers who are activists are often prevented by their work from assuming the role of primary caretaker of their children. Shakur and Kakuya, like Brown and Ericka, are separated shortly after Kakuya's birth. Because Kamau, the child's father, was also incarcerated at the time, Shakur entrusts her mother with Kakuya's care. Shakur poignantly describes the painful consequences for herself of such an early separation. When her four-year-old daughter comes to visit her at the Clinton Correctional Facility in New Jersey, Shakur must contend with the pain of accepting that her daughter does not recognize her as "mother." Shakur writes: "She calls me Mommy Assata and she calls my mother Mommy" (258). She is further tormented by the daughter's understandable inability to comprehend, at such a young age, why her mother has been kept away from her. The fact that Shakur is so deeply moved by their emotionally wrenching encounter bolsters her determination to obtain her freedom. In the aftermath of her daughter's tearful visit, she states simply but emphatically: "I decide that it is time to leave" (258).

In addition to representing the continuation of struggle, therefore, children also, just as importantly, furnish the *motivation* to struggle. In Shakur's poem, "To My Daughter Kakuya" (259), concern for the daughter's welfare translates into the commitment to work toward creating a better world in which beauty, justice, and freedom will be hers to reap. Like "Affirmation," it is a poem that both celebrates life and attests to Shakur's continuing belief in the redemptive power of struggle. Similarly, Brown's narrative closes with the lyrics of a song written for seven-year-old Ericka: "Oh, Ericka, my little baby, / Ericka, my little child, / Ericka, there is no maybe, / I'll change the world for you / In just a little while" (A Taste, 450). Of course the will to make the world a better place for one's children is not unique to activist women's texts; nonactivist mothers also express this will. What is unique, however, is *activist* women's commitment to organized and collective political struggle as the means.

The testimony of women activists, across historical periods and cross-culturally, reveals the extent to which a woman's status as mother can be and is used against her. No such parallel exists for men who are fathers. The forced separation of women prisoners from their children parallels the separation of slave mothers from their young and also aims toward the same objective, namely breaking the captive's spirit and resistance. The forced separation of Ericka Huggins from her daughter Mai, following hard on the violent murder of her husband John, is illustrative. Huggins, indicted with Bobby Seale on bogus conspiracy charges for the murder of Alex Rackley (an alleged police infiltrator operating out of the New Haven, Connecticut, chapter of the Party), is held in solitary confinement. During Huggins's incarceration, her mother maintains custody of Mai. Brown writes that "Ericka cried about not being with her Mai, though Mrs. Huggins did bring her to visit" (A *Taste*, 202). Frances Carter, who was detained in Niantic prison along with Ericka and Carter's sister, Peggy, gives an account in Hilliard's *This Side of Glory* that captures more poignantly the extent of Huggins's trauma. Frances remembers that while they were awaiting trial for the Alex Rackley murder, "Ericka went through the hardest time. She had already lost her husband, John. Now she was pulled away from her daughter. Sometimes she would be up in the corner somewhere, in a fetal position, crying and pulling her hair out" (Hilliard and Cole, 291). Carter indicates that in time, though, and with some sisterly cajoling, Ericka would always regain her spirited demeanor. Carter, who was herself pregnant at the time of their incarceration, recognized the potential power her condition gave her captors over her. Following the confirmation of her pregnancy, she recalls: "My first emotion was anger—I felt my pregnancy would be something else for them to use. Which it was" (Hilliard and Cole, 291). After the child was born, the police attempted to tap into what they imagined were Carter's maternal instincts in order to extort information from her during interrogation sessions. Presuming that more than anything she wanted to be reunited with her child, they tried to convince her to betray her comrades. Carter recalls: "They wanted to use my baby to get me. But I didn't have that bond with him anyway because I hadn't spent no more than maybe two days with him, and was too weak to even hold him, after going through all that twenty-four-hour ordeal. So it wasn't that I didn't *love* my child, because I did, but I knew he was going to be taken care of by my parents, so for them to want to use *that* didn't mean that much to me" (Hilliard and Cole, 293). Significantly, Carter's statement also points to the way the meaning of love is expanded in activists' texts. For Shakur, Brown, and other activists, to love one's children, family, or community implies a willingness also to sacrifice and struggle for a society, a world worthy of their humanity. To work for freedom and justice is thus a profound expression of love. It is in this context that activist women tend to negotiate their roles as mothers.

While Davis's, Shakur's, and Brown's observations about women's roles and experiences as mothers, partners, and comrades in the Movement reflect a patently feminist sensibility, all three women found problematic any serious association with the larger, predominantly White feminist movement unfolding in the late 1960s and early 1970s. In the face of America's virulent racism, most Black women then, as historically, cast their lot with Black men over White women as preferred political allies. Even as the women's narratives tend to affirm this move, they also explore some of the more troubling consequences for Black women of having to make such a choice.

The women's testimonies suggest that at the time, any sustained preoccupation with gender was often subsumed by the more pressing struggle just to remain alive during the years of the government's massive crackdown on radical activists. Brown, for example, describes the particularly turbulent year of 1969 as a time in the Party when women and men "clung to each other fiercely. We forgot cliques and chauvinism and any bit of internal strife" (A *Taste*, 194). Since women and men shared the experience of racist discrimination to the extent that group identity could easily be forged along these lines, many women and men felt that splintering along gender lines would simply fracture the Movement. Of course, implicit in such a claim is the false assumption that men can have no active role to play in a struggle against gender oppression. In other words, splintering need not have occurred along a strictly male-female divide. Cognizant of the failure of both men and women to understand and confront sexism as a dangerous liability to the struggle, Toni Cade Bambara cautioned: "Men have got to develop some heart and some sound analysis to realize that when sisters get passionate about themselves and their direction, it does not mean they're readying up to kick men's ass. They're readying up for honesty. And women have got to develop some heart and some sound analysis so that they can resist the temptation of buying peace with their man with self-sacrifice and posturing" (Bambara, 109). Unfortunately, many of the women who embraced Bambara's challenge soon became targets of male derision. One means of neutralizing the most assertive was to label them "feminists." The overt resistance Brown claims she encountered as head of the Black Panther Party is paradigmatic. She writes: "A woman attempting the role of leadership was, to my proud black Brothers, making an alliance with the 'counter-revolutionary, man-hating, lesbian, feminist white bitches.' It was a violation of some Black power principle that was left undefined. If a black woman assumed a role of leadership, she was said to be eroding black manhood, to be hindering the progress of the black race. She was an enemy of black people" (A Taste, 357). Since many in the Black community (not without cause) viewed the feminist movement as a phenomenon exclusively relevant to the concerns of White, middle-class women, to be labeled feminist was to be dismissed as a collaborator with privileged White women against the interests of the Black community (generally read as the interests of Black men). Brown notes that her efforts to appoint other women to prominent leadership positions within the Party were met with resistance and hostility (363). Although Brown, Shakur, and Davis indicate that some women did attain high status within the Party (something that set the organization apart from many of the other political organizations that came into being during the era), their influence was often circumscribed by a combination of male privilege and violence. Citing Zayd Shakur as one of a few notable exceptions in her experience, Shakur echoes Brown in referring to the "macho cult that was an official body of the BPP" (Assata, 223).

In describing the way women in leadership positions were often vilified, Brown also makes an important statement about the use of homophobia in conjunction with sexism to restrict women's activities. The rhetoric of the era is illustrative. Homophobic charges of lesbianism were then, as today, wielded against women organizing for self-empowerment. In a similar way, rhetoric conflating masculinity with compulsory heterosexuality was and is invoked as a means of policing men's behavior. For example: in "Notes on a Native Son," from his widely celebrated collection of autobiographical essays, *Soul On Ice*, Eldridge Cleaver makes several virulently homophobic remarks to this end. Brown's recollection of Cleaver's language on one occasion in reference to David Hilliard exemplifies both the antiwoman and antihomosexual impulses that frequently surfaced in the rhetoric of the Movement. After referring to Hilliard as "pussy" for his reluctance to aggressively advance armed struggle within the Party (during the years of Newton's incarceration), Cleaver continues: "Revolution has to be won, not coddled like eggs. The Hilliards are so punked-out and gun-shy, they're making the vanguard look like a reformist bitch" (*A Taste*, 223). Cleaver's gender-charged language denigrates women's bodies, associating femaleness with that which is weak, vile, and detestable. Such exclusion based on sexual orientation marked yet another contradiction within the resistance struggle, since tolerance for selective oppression of one group potentially imperils the freedom of all others. June Jordan puts the matter well in her insistence that "freedom cannot be qualified." She further asserts: "If you were to omit from the American Left all the gay and lesbian people that there are, you would have no Left left" (from the film *A Place of Rage*).

Black women who openly pushed feminist agendas were often at odds with not only Black men, but White women as well. Audre Lorde perceptively differentiates between the political interests and circumstances of Black women and those of the majority of White feminist women. She writes:

> [I]n a patriarchal power system where whiteskin privilege is a major prop, the entrapments used to neutralize Black women and white women are not the same. For example, it is easy for Black women to be used by the power structure against Black men, not because they are men, but because they are Black. Therefore, for Black women, it is necessary at all times to separate the needs of the oppressor from our own legitimate conflicts within our communities. This same problem does not exist for white women. Black women and men have shared racist oppression and still share it, although in different ways. (Lorde, 118)

Chicana writer and feminist theorist Cherríe Moraga nevertheless questions the often out-of-hand rejection of feminism by women of color.

She notes, for instance, the contradiction often evident in the dismissal by women of color of White women's theorizing on gender. Moraga points to the irony in the fact that while Chicano men routinely resort to White theoreticians such as Marx and Engels to advance theories of Chicano oppression, Chicana women are criticized for turning to White women's theorizing to talk about gender (Moraga, 106). Although her comments refer specifically to Chicana women, her analysis might just as easily be applied to African American women as well. Moraga notes that many Chicanas who actually assert a feminist sensibility tend to do so in the context of what she terms an "alongside-our-man-knee-jerk-phenomenon" (107). Any other approach would leave women open to censure from the larger Chicano community. Apologies or qualifications similar to the one Moraga identifies among Chicanas also abound in political narratives by other women of color involved in nationalist struggles. The combination, then, of the pressure to maintain (at least outwardly) racial solidarity with Black men and of alienation from the agenda of the predominantly White, middle-class women's movement account, historically, for Black women's reluctance to identify as feminist. Of course, this debate continues in the contemporary context, with many women of the African Diaspora preferring to call themselves *womanists* (after Alice Walker's coinage) rather than *feminists*. They use the former as a means of distinguishing their particular activist values and concerns from those of White women. Brown's comments in A *Taste* illustrate Moraga's claim: "Like most black women of the time, we considered the notion of women's liberation to be a 'white girl's thing.' Unlike the new feminists, we were not going to take a position against men. Our men did not have to 'change or die,' as the most radical of the feminists were saying. Black men were our Brothers in the struggle for black liberation" (A *Taste*, 192). Brown goes on to insist, however, that Black women "had no intention . . . of allowing Panther men to assign us an inferior role in our revolution" (192). Brown's qualification is addressed by Davis in her 1992 essay, "Black Nationalism: The Sixties and the Nineties." Davis indicates that while White feminism seemed to Black women at the time largely irrelevant, many Black women simultaneously found compulsory male leadership intolerable (Davis, "Black Nationalism," 320).

Ultimately, Brown reevaluates her early dismissal of sexism as an unimportant concern on Black women's agendas. Despite the virulent resistance she encounters upon assuming leadership of the Party, she determines to make women's liberation (as it already existed in theory) a critical addition to Party practice. She writes: "There would be no further impositions on me by men, including black men, including Black Panther men. I would support every assertion of human rights by women—from the right to abortion to the right of equality with men as laborers and leaders. I would declare that the agenda of the Black Panther Party and our revolution to free black people from oppression specifically included black women" (*A Taste*, 368). The change in her stance on women's reproductive freedom is especially significant given the Party's official line, as noted earlier, regarding birth control and abortion.

Finally, Black women's attitudes toward feminism during the era were also complicated by the tension between Black women and White women over Black men. The narratives by Black women supply information not readily found in Black men's texts, including the impact on Black women of Black male fascination and/or preoccupation with White women. Historically victimized by Euroamerican standards of beauty, Black women express pain over Black men's reverence (not always conscious) of White images of beauty. As the era of Black Power ushered in a new aesthetic, Black women found themselves in the peculiar position of being revered as so-called "African queens" by day while many of these same admiring brothers sought the company of White women by night. Many Black women perceived sexual liaisons between White women and Black men not only as personally offensive but also as a threat to the integrity of the struggle. Describing her resentment toward Elaine Wender (the White attorney entrusted with the poems of San Quentin prisoner Johnny Spain), Brown declares: "I really detested the Elaine Wenders of the world. . . . I resented what I felt were their fantasy interests in black people, particularly in black men. Moreover, I detested black men's often unabashed responses to them, to the lifeline they seemed to toss from more comfortable shores" (*A Taste*, 317). Brown recounts a nasty confrontation with Wender after Wender refused to relinquish Spain's poems to the Party. According to her own account,

Brown slapped Wender several times (318). [1] Brown acknowledges in retrospect that her actions on the occasion were extreme; however, she also suggests—not unlike Eldridge Cleaver in *Soul On Ice*—the ways her actions were tied to years of repressed rage and disempowerment. Motivated by more than simply resentment toward White women, Brown maintains that her assault on Wender represented an "act of will in a life of submission" (319).

Despite her hostility toward the "Elaine Wenders of the world," Brown's sexual relationships with Jay Kennedy and Bert Schneider ironically constitute a mere reversal of the Black man-White woman paradigm. Except for fleeting pangs of guilt which she confides to Bunchy Carter, Brown has little to say in retrospect about how her liaisons with wealthy, influential White men were received by her Black fellow activists—male or female—at the time. What she does discuss is the manner in which she apparently wielded her sexuality to temporarily reverse the hierarchy of power between Black women and White men. After having sex with and then securing a sizable contribution from Schneider, for example, to pay a year's advance rent on Newton's penthouse apartment, Brown contemplates the signification of her actions. She writes: "I felt relief rush over me, along with shame. It was not about comrades, certainly not about morality, not even about Huey. I worried that Bert would think I had used him. And perhaps I had. Perhaps not" (264). Brown notes that Newton, impressed by the financial return, later teased her about her "twelve-thousand-dollar pussy" (270). Brown recalls that as part of their orientation into the Party, women recruits were reminded that they might someday be called upon to deploy their sexuality as but another weapon against the enemy (136). Although Brown uses the politics of the Movement to contextualize her various relationships over the years with different White men, her relationship of several years with wealthy French industrialist Peter Elby (also a White man) suggests that her attraction to White men entails more than simply exploitation. Other possibilities, however, are neither proposed nor explored in her narrative. In general, one does not find among Black women's texts the

---

[1] Hugh Pearson recounts considerably different (i.e., from Brown's account in *A Taste*) circumstances precipitating the confrontation between Brown and Wender (Pearson, 256–57).

endeavor to explicate Black female-White male relationships in the same way that Black men's texts have sought to theorize Black male-White female relationships.

As Shakur notes, fascination with White women on the part of some Black men often occurs at the expense of villainizing Black women. She recalls, for instance, that a lot of the Black men she met in Greenwich Village were "hung up" on White women. She writes: "When i asked them why, they said white women are sweeter, Black women are evil; white women are more understanding, Black women are more demanding" (*Assata*, 112). Not only did some Black men's declared preference for and/or veneration of White women as the epitome of femininity undermine Black women's self-esteem, but—hyped as it became by the media—it also threatened to reduce the focus of the liberation struggle of Black people to a bid by Black men for equality with White men based on shared male privilege and equal access to all women's bodies, Black or White. Nowhere is this idea more disturbingly put forward than in Eldridge Cleaver's *Soul On Ice*. In the first chapter, "On Becoming," Cleaver describes how he became an adept rapist by first practicing and perfecting his technique on expendable Black girls in the ghetto. "[A]nd when i considered myself smooth enough," Cleaver concludes, "I crossed the tracks and sought out white prey" (E. Cleaver, 14). In sexually brutalizing White women, in particular, Cleaver imagines himself engaged in an "insurrectionary act" (14) intended foremost to even a score with White men. In a war between subjects (i.e., White and Black men), the women in Cleaver's scheme (which, incidentally, hardly originates with him) figure only as objects of exchange. Rejecting the popular assumption that "the Negro male's lust and desire for the white dream girl is purely an esthetic attraction," Cleaver argues to the contrary, that "his motivation is often of such a bloody, hateful, bitter, and malignant nature that whites would really be hard pressed to find it flattering" (17). Notably, other African American men's autobiographies, including the *Autobiography of Malcolm X* and Chester Himes's *Lonely Crusade*, recount similar ambivalent struggles over the bodies of White women, often culminating in physical and/or emotional abuse. James Baldwin's powerful fictional portrait of the interracial couple, Rufus (an African American man) and Leona (a White woman) in his 1960 novel, *Another Country*, supplies a dimension missing from these autobiographies. Expanding his analysis beyond the politics of race, Baldwin implicitly interrogates the extent to which the social construction of masculinity under patriarchy works to render such unions destructive for both parties involved. In the same way that White men historically justified the brutalizing of Black men with the rationale that they were protecting the honor of White women, Cleaver justifies his raping of White women as an act of revenge on behalf of Black women. In both instances, the women themselves are reduced to pawns, stripped of agency and voice. Although Cleaver both reevaluates and renounces his early thinking on the matter, his analysis of his mindset at the time draws exclusively on the psychosexual dynamics of racist oppression under White supremacy (as explicated by Frantz Fanon, for example, in *Black Skin, White Masks*) without ever considering the politics of gender. His retrospective critique of his past actions essentially ignores the counterrevolutionary implications of his longing for acceptance into and full participation in the dominant patriarchal order.

Ideologically poised at the intersection of the Black Power and feminist movements, the autobiographies by Davis, Shakur, and Brown draw attention to the ways in which the nationalist rhetoric of Cleaver and others often translated into oppressive practices that victimized women. In exposing some of the internal contradictions around gender that threatened to compromise the Movement as a fight for liberation from all forms of oppression, the women's narratives document not just the objective "fact" of sexism as a problem within the Movement, but the "truth" of its material and psychological impact on Black women, something largely unaccounted for in the men's texts even as many claimed to object to the perpetuation of oppressive gender practices. In reading the women's narratives in conjunction with the men's, one sees that women often experienced interaction with the dominant culture, parenthood, intimate relationships, and the quest for self-determination in significantly different ways from their male counterparts. In the end, the failure to account for this difference not only strained communication and solidarity between women and men, but as Bambara argued, also threatened to undermine the cohesiveness of the Movement at its most fundamental level.

While all three women's narratives provide critical insight into gender dynamics during the era, Brown's autobiography, published nearly two decades after her association with the Party, is especially compelling for its simultaneous unveiling of the psychosexual dynamics of power in 1960s-1970s Black nationalist struggle. Brown's revelations challenge any gender-essentialist assumptions that would posit the potential to abuse power as a solely masculine phenomenon. Brown's detailed disclosures about sexism in the Party, about her own sexual escapades, and about the personal lives of other activists have drawn sharp criticism from her detractors. Her candor extends well beyond mention of repressive gender and sexual politics within the Party, to include frank discussion of egregious abuses of power that transpired within the organization's ruling circle and the psychosexual dimensions characterizing this abuse. Indeed, the nature and extent of Brown's disclosures about the sordid internal affairs of the Black Panther Party are unrivaled by any autobiographical text from or about the period to date.

Some critics have charged that Brown is relatively silent on matters concerning abuses of power that transpired under her own leadership. Kathleen Cleaver also argues that Brown misrepresents the extent to which her close association with Huey Newton made her complicit in many of the Party's more unsavory activities. A cursory read of *A Taste* will surely miss, though, subtle moments in which Brown *is* critical of her own past actions. Repeatedly noting the way the Party came to define her identity, Brown admits to fear of severing her ties precisely because to do so would lead to a loss of self. There are moments in the text in which she is decidedly but subtly critical of her own motivations for adhering to questionable Party practices and dogma. Describing her own conditioned indifference to Newton's violent "disciplining" of Party members, Brown compares herself to a soldier no longer emotionally affected by the sight of blood or brutality. She writes: "I had become hardened to such things, like a Green Beret who learns to think nothing of taking a life: after seeing so many training films on brutal killings he is no longer repulsed by blood or brutality" (*A Taste*, 9). In yet another instance, she is very candid about the extent of her complicity in neglecting to challenge such practices. She rationalizes, for instance, Newton's brutal battering of his tailor, Preston Callins, in her presence. Callins, who presented at the hospital with four depressed skull fractures, required neurosurgery as a result of the beating (Coleman with Avery, 35). Brown allows the reader insight into her thinking at the time. She explains: "I had come to believe everything would balance out in the revolutionary end. I also knew that being concerned about Callins was too costly, particularly in terms of my position in the party. Yes, I thought, fuck Callins" (*A Taste*, 7). In retrospect, Brown acknowledges her willed blindness to the happenings around her. At the time, however, she refused to see Newton's increasing violence and irrational episodes directed at other Party members until this violence was turned on her. Journalist Renée Graham notes that "Brown admits she was often protected from the worst mistreatment [inside the Party], first by [Bunchy] Carter, then by Newton after he was released from prison in 1970" (Graham, 32). Brown chose merely to adopt Newton's sentiment toward Callins and others as her own. She is critical of her own thinking (highlighting in the above passage her primary concern for self-preservation over the welfare of all others), but still—as is repeatedly the case throughout the narrative—avoids present judgment of her past actions. Brown's peculiar style of narrating, which seems strategically to avoid situating a present "I" in her text, makes it possible for her to evade personal accountability as she represents her past actions. Because of this style of narration, her text is less itself an explicit critique of power dynamics in the Party than a presentation of episodes that *invite* such critique. That is, while Brown's repeated allusions to the relationship between sex and power point to disturbing psychosexual dimensions of certain Party practices, readers are left to interpret for themselves the implications of the episodes she recounts. Even so, the unique insight to be gained into the Party, the era, and the nature of power itself from reading *A Taste* marks Brown's narrative as an important instance of political witnessing.

As Brown notes, sexual openness was part of the spirit of the times. Having sex during the era, she writes, was "akin to drinking water" in terms of the casualness with which individuals experimented with different sexual partners (*A Taste*, 107). Brown captures well the sense in which activists' acute awareness of their own mortality (the result of surviving under violent repression and of witnessing death repeatedly) led them to live fully in the present. Fellow Panther Masai Hewit, for instance, marvels with Brown over their having endured together six funerals in just six months' time (195). Brown places the sexual openness and intimacy between men and women during the era in the context of war; sexual expression was one means of celebrating life against a backdrop of impending danger and devastating loss. Nevertheless, Brown's disclosure of intimate details about her sexuality is paradigmatic of the kind of personal details largely absent in the autobiographies of other women activists. She recalls, for instance—in various degrees of detail—sexual affairs and encounters with at least twelve Party men, apart from her long-standing relationship with Huey Newton. The ethics of naming her lovers aside (many of whom were married or otherwise "committed" to others at the time), critics have noted that the sexual episodes described in A *Taste* give the narrative a racy, novelistic appeal. Is it merely sensationalism, though, that prompts Brown to include such highly personal details? Of course, that cannot be ruled out in a culture where sex is regularly marketed for profit by print, television, and film media. However, to read these episodes solely in terms of their sensational value is to miss other important issues raised by their inclusion. In many ways, Brown's disclosures further our understanding of social dynamics and gender relations during the era. Additionally, her frankness about her own experiences acknowledges and affirms Black female sexuality and desire. Perhaps most compelling, however, is the extent to which Brown's sexual disclosures invite a fundamentally new approach to reading and understanding the nature of power as it operated within the Black Power Movement and as it operates in American society more broadly.

Brown's frankness about sexual matters challenges negative silences around Black female sexuality. Her identification of herself as a sexual being is a radical move in a society where Black women's sexuality is almost always overdetermined. Because racist ideology historically has marked Black women's bodies as hypersexed, many Black women choose to silence or minimize the sexual aspect of their identity so as not to fuel existing stereotypes. Against both the cultural dictates about the impropriety of women talking about or initiating or enjoying sex, and enduring racist assumptions about Black women as hypersexed, Brown is unapologetic about her own sexual desire and experiences. Her openness to sharing this part of herself is indicated by the details she supplies about intimate encounters with different men. Her description of making love with Larry is illustrative. Brown writes: "His toughness was tender, I thought enveloped in his body, which was full and fit and dark and sweet. He made love with fire, a smoldering, satisfying heat. I caressed his muscular buttocks as we lay in the dark and dreamed out loud" (*A Taste*, 402). The detailed passage presents Brown as an unapologetically sexual being. Interestingly, it also inverts conventional paradigms in which men usually describe and appraise the physical attributes of women. Rather than minimizing her sexual experiences, then, Brown insists upon their being seen as part of who she is. Even if Brown's self-revelations are partially motivated by a desire to undercut the potential for her detractors (both inside and outside of the Movement) to use this information against her (a vulnerability peculiar to women), Brown's inclusion of such details works to affirm Black female sexuality as normal and healthy. Her articulation of the formerly unarticulated also widens a space in which Black women can talk critically about their experiences in a climate less laden with shame and censure. Because Brown is critical at many points of the nature of some of her sexual encounters, she portrays herself alternately as sexual subject and object, noting the empowering aspects of the former and the dehumanizing tendency of the latter.

What is most compelling about Brown's treatment of sex and sexuality in *A Taste*, however, is the way power (often expressed as violence) is eroticized. For Brown, having and exercising power (i.e., the capacity to have one's communicated intentions met with acquiescence) is sensual. She confesses: "It was a sensuous thing to know that at one's will an enemy can be struck down, a friend saved. The corruption in that affirmation coexists comfortably with the sensuousness and the seriousness of it" (319). Even the title she chooses for her autobiography, *A Taste of Power*, renders power in sensual terms. Brown's illustrations of the internecine violence that eventually destroyed the Party repeatedly point toward not only sexual but sadomasochistic underpinnings with important implications.

Although neither the term nor the practice of sadomasochism is explicitly invoked in Brown's narrative, her rendering of a clearly sadomasochistic episode early in the autobiography (prior to her association with the Party) almost invites us to read other incidents recounted in her text through this lens. Shortly after her arrival in California at the age of twenty-five, Brown's naive participation as a Dominatrix in a sadomasochistic ritual becomes a symbolic trying on of power. Lured by the prospect of securing quick cash with seemingly little personal investment, Brown is, by her own admission, duped into meeting a man whom she is instructed to physically chastise. She writes: "He hurriedly took off his clothes, while I remained, as instructed, in mine: tight black pants, black turtleneck sweater, and high-heeled black shoes. . . . He threw his huge naked fleshiness onto my convertible bed and begged me to beat him. I grabbed the belt and simply whipped him, as though I had done it before" (74). Before Brown is paid for her "services," however, the client makes a hasty departure, promising to come right back after removing his car from a no-parking zone. When he fails to return, Brown realizes that she is the one who has been the "trick." The client's seeming subjugation to her will is exposed as illusory. Reading Brown's text allegorically through this particular episode has significant implications, as the episode parallels the manner in which she is eventually given leadership of the Black Panther Party. Her status vis-à-vis the Party is similar to that of the Dominatrix in that the extent of her power is rigorously circumscribed by the wishes of another. Since the authority Brown is permitted to exercise over the organization emanates from Huey Newton, Newton always retains the power to usurp control at any time. As with the Dominatrix, then, Brown's power is merely "a taste."

In *Sadomasochism in Everyday Life*, Lynn Chancer suggests that any hierarchical social structure potentially yields sadomasochistic dynamics. The Party's very structure thus doomed it to recapitulate many of the same power dynamics at work in the dominant culture. Brown, in fact, acknowledges that it was the Party's rigidly authoritarian paramilitary structure that enabled her to realize power within the organization. She explains: "Within a chapter were branches, organized by city, and within the branches were sections. These were divided into subsections, which were divided into squads. Ideas and information flowed up and down the chain of command. Orders went from the top to the bottom" (*A Taste*, 135). Such a structure ensured respect for her authority, even as her gender was often resented by the predominantly male membership consigned to follow her orders. Certainly the exploitative nature of economic and social relations under capitalism and patriarchy, in general, provide an ideal context for the emergence of sadomasochistic dynamics. Chancer proposes that "Rather than sadomasochism being merely the property of individuals, [American capitalist] culture itself is deeply oriented in a sadomasochistic direction. We are living in a society sadomasochistic in that it bombards us with experiences of domination and subordination far more regularly than it exposes us to sensations and inklings of freedom and reciprocity" (Chancer, 2). In *A Taste*, Brown illustrates the fluidity between the positions of sadist and masochist, noting her own passage through both roles. In the role of sadist, Brown acknowledges ordering and supervising the vicious beating of Steve, a fellow Panther who allegedly challenged her authority. Once a victim of Steve's physical abuse herself, Brown admits that this motivated her desire to see him punished for his flagrant disrespect for her authority. In an analeptic narrative moment, she recounts her retaliation against Steve: "I had not intended committing an act of vengeance. Despite my memory of the fists that had brutalized my body a few years before, there were larger issues involved when I ordered Steve to Oakland" (368). She seems to make the latter assertion as an attempt to convince herself, simultaneously providing the reader insight into her own rationalizing of the incident at the time. Further, in asserting that she "had not intended committing an act of vengeance," she implicitly concedes that this is, in fact, what she did. Repeatedly, Brown's recollections of her own actions as titular head of the Party remind us that the capacity to abuse power is a non-gender-specific phenomenon.

In the role of masochist, Brown admits to a dependence on and need for validation from others to escape feelings of emptiness, learned self-hatred, and nonexistence. Her ascension to power in the Party allows her to shed the role of masochist. Recalling her address to an assembly of Panthers she summoned in order to announce her new position as head of the Party, Brown writes that "there was something in that moment that seemed a reparation for all the rage and pain of my life" (6).

In invoking a sadomasochistic paradigm to talk about power relations within the Party, I wish to stress that the plight of the masochist is defined less by pleasure in subordination (which would be highly problematic in speaking about oppression) than by psychological or material dependence. Certainly, the nature of this dependence has been thoughtfully documented in the works of Frantz Fanon (*The Wretched of the Earth*) and Albert Memmi (*The Colonizer and the Colonized*), among other studies. Dependence on the Party, once members became deeply involved and committed to its vision, almost guaranteed submission to the range of the Party's activities, including some of its more unsavory practices. After all, committing oneself to the Party generally involved profound sacrifice, both personal (alienation from one's family as well as the society at large) and financial (members turned over any individual income to the collective, and in turn lived communally with other Party members). Acknowledging his desire to leave the Party long before he was eventually expelled, David Hilliard reflects, for example: "But where am I going to go? By myself I am nothing but obligations I can't possibly meet. Plus, leaving the Party will endanger me: I face years in prison and can't afford my own lawyer. Besides, my legal battles come from working with the Party. To fight on my own would be suicide. I've never wanted to leave the Party more; but there's no place to go" (Hilliard and Cole, 309). On another level, for some activists, including Brown by her own admission, membership in the Party provided for the first time a sense of purpose and meaningful identity. Since the sadomasochistic dynamic is never static, the stakes are always being raised. Any increase in resistance from the dominated is always met with an increase in abuse/tyranny from the dominator. Only when the dominated succeed in leaving the situation, as both Hilliard and Brown (among others) eventually did, can the sadomasochistic dynamic be broken.

Brown notes that prior to actually joining the organization, she, like many who witnessed the Panthers in action, was impressed by the spirit of resistance and self-determination the Party exuded. As Angela Davis notes, the Panthers provided a "romantic revolutionary image" at the same time that they promoted active resistance. Style was an important part of their allure and thus a useful strategy in mobilizing communities of resistance (*A Place of Rage*). Of course, style in general was highly politicized during the era. The hippie movement, the cultural nationalists, and the Black Panthers all had their own unique dress styles vis-à-vis mainstream America, each connoting a particular brand of politics. The Panthers' habitual donning of black leather (the official Party uniform) is just one example of an accouterment often associated with sadomasochistic sexual practice. As many have testified, much of the Party's immediate appeal to the uninitiated, in fact, had to do with their distinctive appearance, notably the black leather, the dark shades, the open display of weaponry, the use of military formations, and the aura of power associated with all four. The mixture of awe and fear the Panthers regularly inspired might be read as arising in part from the (unconscious) cultural fascination and titillation with the paraphernalia of sadomasochism, signifying as it does the forbidden or unknown—specifically, lawlessness and the deliberate transgressing of (sexual) taboos.

A much more disturbing manifestation of sadomasochism Brown describes, however, is the Black Panther Party's use of whips in administering corporal punishment, a practice ironically evocative of the historical experience of slavery. According to Brown, "disciplining" generally entailed being lashed across the back with a whip (A *Taste*, 275). Contrary to slaves, however, Party members willingly submitted to authoritarian rule and discipline on account of their own commitment to and belief in the ideals of the organization. The analogy to a sadomasochistic paradigm here is instructive. As Chancer indicates: "both sadist and masochist remain rigidly within the parameters of their respective roles; they are symbiotically interdependent; and the masochist has been forcibly restricted in such a way that challenging sadomasochistic intercourse (literally or figuratively) is . . . only possible under certain rules of the game that do not ever really allow the power of the sadist to be challenged" (Chancer, 11). Brown's account of the violent expulsion of then Party Chairman Bobby Seale reveals that even members of the central committee (with the exception of Newton) were not exempt from the practice of disciplining. Brown's account of Seale's expulsion, during one of Newton's drug-induced rages in the latter years of the Party, is chilling. Brown writes that Newton became offended when Seale repeated a third party's criticism of Newton's leadership. Though Seale insisted that he avidly defended Newton to his detractor, Newton was not appeased and continued to escalate the confrontation until the scene culminated in the violent lashing of Seale with a bullwhip. From her position as voyeur, Brown recalls: "Though a relatively thin man, Bobby bent only slightly with each lash, his head down, eyes tight, braced for the next crack. I remained at the table, smoking" (A *Taste*, 351). Although Brown places five other Party members at the scene, none of them (including Brown) makes an effort to avert what all apparently recognized as an unprovoked and unjust attack on Seale. Each rightly assumed, no doubt, that such violence could just as easily be turned on them.

As graphic as Brown's account of Seale's expulsion in the autobiography is, it merely hints, by other accounts, at the extent to which sadomasochistic practices allegedly were carried out within the Party. Hugh Pearson's 1994 study, *The Shadow of the Panther: The Price of Black Power in America*, for instance, proposes an even more troubling account of the circumstances surrounding Seale's expulsion. In his interviews with former Party member Mary Kennedy (on August 29, 1992 in Oakland) and with one-time Panther sympathizer David Horowitz (on October 6, 1992 in Los Angeles), Kennedy and Horowitz maintained that Seale was not only violently beaten but also *sodomized* by Newton on the occasion of his expulsion (Pearson, 264, 391 fn.).[2] Pearson writes that "Newton dramatically beat Seale with a bullwhip and sodomized him so violently that his anus had to be surgically repaired by a physician who was a party supporter" (264). Pearson further notes that Horowitz "provides written confirmation for the sodomizing in [the] article 'Black Murder, Inc.,' by David Horowitz, *Heterodoxy*, March 1993" (391 fn.). Seale has denied not only that he was sodomized, but also that he was even beaten. Oddly, his 1978 autobiography, *A Lonely Rage*, omits any mention at all of the July 1974 expulsion. By his own account, Seale left the Party without incident and of his own volition. When confronted (in the aftermath of *A Lonely Rage*'s publication) by reporter Kate Coleman with contrary testimony and evidence from other Party members, Seale adamantly denied that he was beaten and further charged that the rumors were likely the result of a disinformation campaign initiated by the police. When Coleman indicated that her sources included someone who claimed to have actually treated his injuries, Seale allegedly screamed into the phone: " 'What injuries? . . . I had no injuries whatsoever! I don't give a damn who said it. Tell them I said they're a flat black-ass, motherfucking liar, or a white-assed liar—whoever the hell they are' " (Coleman with Avery, 33). The tenor of Seale's extreme denial (i.e., extreme in the sense that nobody but he seems to deny the fact that he was at least expelled), as well as the bizarre nature of the charge itself, suggests that, at the very least, something traumatic transpired to cause Seale's abrupt departure from the Party. Given Newton's history of incarceration (and

---

[2] Mary Kennedy joined the Party in 1968 and left in 1973, disillusioned by its apparent deterioration. David Horowitz, who became associated with the Party after 1971, left disgruntled in the aftermath of Betty Van Patter's mysterious disappearance and murder.

therefore, probable exposure to sodomy as an expression of violence and debasement among prisoners), as well as the Party's documented practice of corporal punishment as a disciplinary measure, Pearson's claim is not unfathomable. Assuming there *was* more to the episode than just the beating Brown's narrative recounts, Brown's decision to omit further detail could be out of a desire to protect the image of the Party, herself, or both. Several disparaging remarks about Seale in the narrative (she not only raises questions about his intelligence, but criticizes his general ineffectiveness as a leader [A *Taste*, 273] and mocks several of his ideas— his cleanliness campaign, for example [347]) make it seem unlikely that Brown would have been interested in protecting *Seale's* image by deliberately omitting such detail. Furthermore, the suppression of sensitive information is hardly consistent with other moments in the narrative where Brown is quite candid in disclosing others' intimate secrets (her naming of former lovers and her treatment of Kathleen Cleaver as a victim of domestic violence being paradigmatic). It appears that Brown's omission is a calculated one. Disclosing the sodomizing of Seale (as if the beating alone were not damning enough) would not only have further damaged romantic images of the Party, but would have even more deeply implicated Brown herself as a participant in the sadomasochistic dynamics that her narrative intimates were common, especially since there is no indication in the autobiography that Brown subsequently sought to distance herself from Newton's inner circle. The incident points again to Brown's own oscillation between the roles of sadist and masochist, or victimizer and victim, as the circumstances portend.

Brown's eventual break with the Party is also marked by what might be described as sadomasochistic violence. In A *Taste*, Brown indicates that Newton's increasing paranoia, which eventually alienated most of those closest to him, led her to believe that it would not be long before she, too, would become the victim of one of his irrational purges (353). Weary over Newton's failure to seriously address sexist violence against women and its negative impact on Party morale, and fearing that matters would only get worse, Brown claims that she determined to flee for her own safety. As in the case of her description of Seale's departure, however, other sources suggest a slightly different chain of events than what Brown recalls in the autobiography. Hugh Pearson maintains that just prior to her departure, Brown was brutally battered by Newton to the extent that she required hospitalization for her injuries (Pearson, 281, 395 fn.). Although Brown notes that she was once slapped by Newton (*A Taste*, 9), there is clearly no mention in *A Taste* of any assault this severe. In fact, in recounting the incident (which she describes as "commonplace inside our dangerous ranks"), Brown writes: "He struck me. It was a slap in my face after I had made an innocuous remark. Huey had not so much as raised his voice in anger to me prior to that, not even in that last month, when the snares of his madness had left so many others maimed" (9). Brown's minimizing/omission of the beating is ironic, especially given her rather condescending portrait of Kathleen Cleaver elsewhere in her text. That is, rather than choosing to distance herself from Cleaver in the narrative, Brown might have used her own circumstance to express the kind of feminist solidarity her text argues for.

While it is true, as other sources have charged, that Brown repeatedly fails to explore the full implications of many of her own disclosures about abuses of power within the BPP, her narrative nevertheless opens the door to public discussions about the organization and its operations (particularly during its later years) that have not—and perhaps, as Angela Davis argues, could not have—taken place prior to the 1990s. As late as his own study, Hugh Pearson admits that he had difficulty finding ex-Panthers willing to talk critically about Huey Newton and the Party. He writes: "The horrific truth of the party's downfall was an open secret among black Oaklanders and party veterans, but most of them insisted on silence (and still do to this day)—something akin to not discussing the state of a relative who has gone to pot, or, sensing that death might occur any day, preparing to recall only the best" (Pearson, 292). The lack of respondents forthcoming meant that Pearson was left to rely, for his own study, primarily on individuals openly disillusioned about both their own experiences within the Party and the direction the organization eventually took. Bob Blauner's review of *The Shadow of the Panther* (Blauner, 22) indicates that seven of Pearson's twenty-eight interviewees requested anonymity as a condition for their input.

Pearson fails to note, however, that activists' reluctance to talk likely also arises from their awareness of how such testimony can be and often is politically manipulated to reduce, undermine, and/or dismiss the Movement in its entirety without appreciation for its complexity or achievements above and beyond whatever serious shortcomings also existed. It is in this context that Brown's own revelations must be considered. Even as Brown remains guarded in her confessions, the fact that she writes her autobiography in a different sociopolitical climate as well as from the psychological advantage of greater retrospective distance than either Davis or Shakur means that she enjoys greater freedom to confront potentially explosive internal issues. In seizing this freedom, Brown creates with her narrative new spaces for important discussions about gender and sexual politics, and about power dynamics in nationalist struggle that, to date, have been only cursorily explored in other activists' works from the period. In the end, contrary to what some of her critics have proposed, Brown's disclosure of explicit information about her own sexuality and illustrations of the psychosexual dynamics at work in the Party suggest a complex relationship between sex, violence, and power that is more instructive than gratuitous. Notwithstanding the sensationalism such revelations lend to her narrative, Brown participates, no less than the other activist writers whose ranks she joins, in an important kind of political witnessing. The issues presented in her narrative complement and expand the critiques offered by Davis and Shakur. Taken collectively, their narratives not only provide insight into the gender and power dynamics at work during the Black Power Movement, but also impart valuable lessons for how activists today might theorize and wage contemporary resistance struggles.

Chapter 6

Reading Intertextually
Black Power Narratives
Then and Now

Perhaps the most rewarding aspect of reading the autobiographies published over the last two decades by Black Power activists is the extent to which the texts appear collectively to converse with each other, as well as with their anticipated readership. That is, the critical gaze of the writers is focused not only externally, but also internally, on the dynamics inside the Movement. Within the Movement, the women talk to the men, for example, while later narratives often challenge the recollections of accounts published earlier. Sometimes the intertextual dialogue is explicit (as when Davis engages George Jackson or when Kathleen Cleaver takes issue with Brown); other times this dialogue is implicit (as when Hilliard rereads Eldridge Cleaver or gives us a new perspective for understanding Huey Newton). In the end, the accretion of information and stories reiterated about a shared cast of characters over the same period results in a rich, polyvocal *people's* history of the Movement. It is a history that deconstructs itself to reveal many, often irreducible truths as opposed to any monolithic Truth. This final chapter examines how reading activists' narratives intertextually results in a more complex and holistic understanding of the Black Power Movement's internal dynamics. This examination begins with attention to the dialogues between women's and men's narratives about gender dynamics within the Movement. It concludes with a look at how two more recent texts, Elaine Brown's *A Taste of Power* and David Hilliard's *This Side of Glory*, participate in revising earlier texts by other writers.

As noted in chapter 5, Davis's, Shakur's, and Brown's narratives effectively highlight troubling contradictions around gender that often marked women's experiences in the struggle. What the women write about sexual politics and gender-role expectations, about the tension between nationalist rhetoric and women's struggle for self-determination, and about contradictions between revolutionary rhetoric and counterrevolutionary practice inevitably results in noteworthy dialogical moments between their narratives and those of male fellow activists like George Jackson, Huey Newton, Bobby Seale, Eldridge Cleaver, and David Hilliard.

Although many of the narratives by men written about or during the same period also raise sexism in the Movement as an issue, their treatment of the subject is often superficial or inadequate. Bobby Seale's 1978 autobiography, A Lonely Rage, is a fitting example. Despite his criticisms of sexism as it manifested itself inside the Party, Seale's text is rife with contradictions as far as women are concerned. Repeatedly, the actions he recounts seem to speak louder than his words. For example, although he talks of the need to relate to women in the Party as partners/comrades in the struggle, more often than not his mention of different women in the autobiography corresponds to their role as past, present, or prospective bedfellows. While Seale asserts that by 1968 women were actually the majority in the Party—making up about 60 percent of the membership (Seale, Rage, 177), Brown's recollections in A Taste contrast markedly with this claim. According to her, during roughly this same period (circa 1968–69), "it was not unusual to see very few women at a [Panther] gathering. There was a low ratio of women to men in L.A. and, really, everywhere in our paramilitary organization" (A Taste, 190). In Seale's narrative, women are almost never mentioned in regard to their political work as strategizers, decision makers, or even organizers. Instead, their contribution to Party activities seems limited to the more mundane secretarial and domestic tasks of typing, photocopying, note-taking, and cooking for Party gatherings. The women who did this work and were also on the front lines as activists in their own right (as opposed to merely companions of men in the struggle) are almost never mentioned, although the texts by Davis, Shakur, and Brown bear witness to their presence. Furthermore, many of the sexual episodes Seale recounts in A Lonely Rage seem gratuitous and self-aggrandizing. Perhaps the most egregious example goes on for three consecutive pages, as he recalls having sex with five different women in a single night. One of these episodes even includes a detailed description of a ménage à trois.

Although, as in Brown's narrative, such explicit accounts of sexual escapades capture one aspect of the quality of men's and women's interaction in the Party and during the era in general, Seale's narrative does not problematize the sexualizing of power (and therefore, the politics of sexuality) the way Brown's text does. Seale often portrays himself as an irresistible stud to whom women are continually drawn, maintaining, for instance, that "All over the country sisters wanted to stay with me. I know some of it was because I was chairman, but some was because I was standing up for them" (Seale, *Rage*, 177). Seale's alleged "standing up" for women, however, does not seem to carry over into his narrative treatment of them. Even as he claims to be critical of the objectification and/ or demeaning of women, he himself participates in this objectification through the quality of his descriptions of encounters with different Party women. Even his description of Leslie, his longtime companion, comes off somewhat flat. Although he describes their union as a "revolutionary love affair" (noting his attraction to Leslie, in part, for her shared ability to "expound and also understand the philosophy of a revolutionary way of life" [223]), she is treated in the end as just another girlfriend rather than as a comrade. When early one morning Seale arbitrarily decides (unbeknownst to Leslie) that it is time for both of them to abandon the Party, she blindly follows behind him without the benefit of any explanation or discussion as to why they are leaving or where they are headed. Although praised earlier by Seale as a woman with a mind of her own, she readily not only abandons her political work with the Party on a whim but also hastily leaves behind her son (in the care of Seale's parents). Awakened from her sleep by Seale, Leslie follows along confused and whimpering, while Seale issues a series of orders. He writes: "Leslie, now hurriedly dressing, looked at me with a worried expression. 'What's the matter, why we getting up like this?' 'Look.' I was stern in the face. 'Just get dressed, get the kids' clothes, and don't do nothing or say anything to wake anybody. Do what I say now, you hear?' 'Ok,' Leslie whimpered, shaking her head, wearing a rather frightened look" (235). Of course, Seale's entire account of how he leaves the Party in *A Lonely Rage* is disputed by other sources, notably Brown's autobiography and Pearson's *Shadow of the Panther*. Seale never mentions Newton's purging of activists from the Party during the organization's later years, but instead ties his reasons for leaving to the longing for a house of his own—a prominent motif throughout his text.

Seale's ultimately infantilizing portrait of Leslie in the autobiography is repeated in his descriptions of Artie, his first wife, from whom he is eventually estranged. Artie's childlike qualities, as described by Seale, render her endearing but not a woman meant to be taken seriously. While Seale discusses political strategy as he and Artie sit in an L.A. cafe, for example, Artie is described as playfully downing a glass of milk, giggling and seemingly oblivious to the seriousness of Seale's conversation. He writes of her: "An even, white film mustache covered her upper lip as she finished with a satisfying 'Ahhhhh!' Setting the glass down and smiling at me, letting me know that she enjoyed the meal and especially the last finishing touch. 'How long we going to stay down here?' She licked her tongue out, wiping the milk moustache off her lip" (172). Despite rhetoric to the contrary, the women in Seale's narrative come off mostly as mindless creatures in need of direction, sex, and parenting from men. And Seale's mark of sensitivity is apparently that he takes seriously the responsibility to satisfy such needs.

Read against A Lonely Rage, Brown's narrative points to even more disturbing evidence of Seale's inconsistency in theory and practice with regard to women. Brown recalls, for example, Seale's demeaning treatment of a young Black woman (around fifteen years old, according to Brown) named Marsha in front of a gathering of several male Party members. When Seale asks Marsha to recite what a brother has to do to "get some" [sex] from her, she responds on cue: "First of all . . . [he's] got to be a Panther. He's got to be able to recite the ten-point platform and program, and be ready to off the pig and die for the People. . . . Can't no motherfucker get no pussy from me unless he can get down with the party" (A Taste, 189). When subsequently asked what qualities a sister ought to exude, by comparison, Marsha dutifully notes that in addition to knowing the ten-point platform and program, and how to shoot and cook, a sister "has to give up the pussy when the Brother is on his job and hold it back when he's not. 'Cause Sisters got pussy power" (189). Her own outrage notwithstanding, Brown notes that Marsha's recitation was enthusiastically rewarded by the men, who laughed and cheered her on. After witnessing the episode with Seale and Marsha, Brown comments sarcastically on the way the word "sister" from the mouths of men in the Party was sounding more and more like "bitch" (190). As if to exemplify the extent to which stories about the Movement remain highly contested, Seale has since vigorously argued that Brown's recounting of this incident is a gross distortion of what actually transpired. Although Seale maintains in his autobiography that he personally labored to establish a nonsexist environment in the Oakland chapter by continually challenging sexist practices (ironically, he specifically cites his disapproval of the use of emotional coercion by men to get women to submit to sex [*Rage*, 177], and of men's assumption that the jobs of cooking and cleaning should be automatically delegated to women [178]), Brown recalls that the sexism she encountered in the Oakland branch was far more virulent than anything going on in L.A. (*A Taste*, 191). Notably, Brown's recollections of pervasive sexism and machismo within the Oakland branch circa 1969 (189–91) also revise (by contradicting) Shakur's assessment (*Assata*, 205) following her visit to the west coast at roughly the same time.

Just as Brown's recollections challenge Seale's on the issue of sexism in the Movement, Davis's narrative calls into question George Jackson's reading of gender in *Soledad Brother*. Jackson's autobiography is unique among political narratives by activists of the period for its epistolary form. Jackson's text is consequently less susceptible to the revisionism of memory—or the rewriting of past experiences through present consciousness. Jackson's autobiography, more so than Davis's, Brown's, or Shakur's, chronologically illustrates (as opposed to narrates) Jackson's move through changing levels of political consciousness. Jackson's early letters to his parents are very different in tone and character from the later ones; many of the early letters are sarcastic, condescending, and dogmatic, especially as they are removed from the immediate context of his family's responses to him. In a December 1, 1967, letter to his father, for instance, Jackson writes: "Dear Robert, I guess there is something to be said for a person who does as he is told, lives by the routine set up by his self-appointed bosses, etc. And of course we must learn to fight our own battles. This way we can die alone, one at a time. This is a very old and proven idea. . . . My trouble is that I have expected too much of you. You're already doing your best: what you feel is right. How can I expect more?" (Jackson, *Soledad*, 117). Jackson's sarcasm in pretending to appreciate ideals he obviously holds in contempt is a biting critique of the kinds of values Robert has either passively or actively assumed as his own. When Jackson claims that there is something to be said for a person who does as he is told and merely adheres to routines established by *self-appointed* bosses, he obviously is not admiring of such qualities. To the contrary, such a person, in Jackson's eyes, cannot live as a human being, but only as a slave. By constantly exposing the contradictions between bourgeois aphorisms and the socioeconomic reality for the majority of urban poor, Jackson attempts to make his family conscious of the ways in which the oppressed can be made to give consent to their own oppression. In order to affirm his own humanity, Jackson is necessarily relentless in recasting the culture's terms of debate. As with other activists, his insistence upon redefining criminality is perhaps the most salient example.

Jackson's work in raising his family's political consciousness is clearly dialogical; however, the disadvantage of the narrative's epistolary form is that half of the dialogue elicited is elided. Of course, it is possible in most instances to simply infer the comments of his correspondents from the content of Jackson's own letters. Even though he perseveres despite their disapproval, the apparent failure of Jackson's family to understand the dynamics of racist, capitalist oppression (even as they themselves are victimized by the same forces) or to appreciate his efforts to resist these forces is a great source of pain, frustration, and anger for him. A letter to Robert, dated November 1967, is illustrative. Jackson writes: "I never realized that I was a source of embarrassment to you, I thought most blacks, especially those of our economic level, understood, vaguely at least, that these places [jails] were built with us in mind, just as were the project houses, unemployment offices, and bible schools. . . . Your inability to understand and support me puts me at a loss, but I cannot allow this to influence my course. I must follow my mind. There is no turning back from awareness" (Jackson, *Soledad*, 115). Although Jackson suggests, at the close of this letter, his need to terminate the correspondence on account of their ideological impasse, he nevertheless continues to write, seeming, in effect, to take his parents' recalcitrance as a pedagogical challenge. Over time, Jackson reveals a greater sense of compassion for his parents as the outcome of their dialogical exchanges. He begins to understand that they, too, are products of particular historical circumstances, and unlike him, have not acquired the tools to critically challenge the values and assumptions governing their lives. Ironically, prison provides Jackson the first opportunity to do this kind of self-work. As his consciousness changes, so does the tone of the later letters to his family.

Although Jackson is extremely perceptive in his analyses of the dynamics of racist oppression, he is initially less attentive to the reality of gender oppression and its impact on the women in his life. For instance, in an October 3, 1967, letter to his mother, Georgia, Jackson indicates that she ought to be more sensitive to Robert's needs and circumstances as an oppressed Black male. He proclaims: "As a sheltered woman, you just do not (and I guess never will) understand what it means to be a man in this particular situation here in the U.S. You just don't suffer the mental mortification of defeat and emasculation that we men do. . . . Imagine how [Robert] must feel when his woman won't even let him run the house" (109). Jackson's reprimand of his mother for her alleged insensitivity toward Robert is ironic given Jackson's own caustic tone toward his father in several of the letters. But even more significant about this passage is the extent to which Jackson privileges the suffering and experiences of his father (and by implication, of Black men in general) over the experiences of his mother (and other Black women in general) under racist *and* sexist oppression. The quality of Georgia Jackson's experiences constitutes a silence in Jackson's text. In a letter to Robert less than two weeks earlier, Jackson encourages his father to more assertively assume the role of patriarch within their family, reminding him that "women and children *enjoy and need* a strong hand poised above them" (108; emphasis added). Not only is Jackson's comment both infantilizing toward women (i.e., the implied comparison of women to children) and presumptuous (he proposes to understand *and* speak for women), but his choice of imagery also ominously sanctions violence as an acceptable means of controlling women.

Because Jackson and Angela Davis were literal correspondents—as a result of Davis's work with the Soledad Defense Committee—and political allies thereafter, their narratives are complementary in many ways. Davis writes: "I came to know George not only through the letters we exchanged, but also through the people who were close to him—through Jon and the rest of the Jackson family" (*Autobiography*, 268). The acknowledgments page to *Soledad Brother* includes mention of Davis. Furthermore, Jackson also shared with Davis the manuscript for *Soledad*

Brother prior to its publication (269). It becomes apparent in both auto-biographies that Davis contributes to Jackson's education and expands his revolutionary consciousness by encouraging him to rethink and re-theorize some of his early sexist views about Black women.

Davis's various references to Jackson, as well as one of her letters to him (reprinted in her narrative), when read against Jackson's letters to her (reprinted in *Soledad Brother*), provide insight into Jackson's intellectual evolution on the issue of gender. Davis notes that Jackson originally viewed Black women as agents of the system (albeit generally unwitting). In *Soledad Brother*, Jackson maintained that Black women, though generally more aggressive than Black men, tended to channel this aggressiveness into succeeding *within* the status quo. Consequently, their focus historically, Jackson argued, had been less on (armed) resistance to the system than on "that 'get a diploma boy' stuff, or 'earn you some money'" (Jackson, *Soledad*, 226). A letter from Davis to Jackson read in court during Davis's trial and strategically incorporated into Davis's narrative offers an insightful defense of this aspect of Black women's behavior in the context of their shared oppression with Black men (*Autobiography*, 371). Davis challenges Jackson's charges of matriarchy and of Black women's complicity in the disempowering of Black men, including Black male children through overprotection of their sons. Both narratives reveal that Jackson's views about Black women ultimately do change. When the women in the House of Detention where Davis is incarcerated acquired contraband copies of the published *Soledad Brother*, Davis writes, they were "exhilarated by the book, but disturbed by [Jackson's] earlier uncomplimentary remarks about Black women" (317). When the women's responses were relayed to Jackson, Davis notes that Jackson "apologized and wanted them all to understand his misjudgment" (317). Davis indicates that Jackson had by that time undergone a metamorphosis in his thinking and was concerned that she inform the women that he no longer subscribed to his earlier generalizations about Black women (62).

In the first of the collected letters (a note to his editor, dated June 1970), Jackson gives a brief chronological account of his life. The short autobiography addresses, in part, the myriad ways in which he, like so many other Black men growing up in America, was systematically prepared and mentally conditioned (by racism and the adverse material circumstances of his life) for eventual entrance into the criminal justice system. "Blackmen," Jackson maintains, "born in the U.S. and fortunate enough to live past the age of eighteen are conditioned to accept the inevitability of prison" (Jackson, *Soledad*, 9). Jackson goes on to assert that his first exposure to this conditioning process came not through interaction with the larger culture but, ironically, from within his own home. He declares: "It always starts with Mama, mine loved me. As testimony of her love, and her fear for the fate of the man-child all slave mothers hold, she attempted to press, hide, push, capture me in the womb. The conflicts and contradictions that will follow me to the tomb started right there in the womb" (9). Addressing Jackson's critique of Black motherhood (evident in the aforesaid passage and voiced at length again in a May 28, 1970, letter to Davis [*Soledad*, 225–27]), Davis counters—in defense of Georgia Jackson and other oppressed Black women—that "to choose between various paths of survival means the objective availability of alternatives." In other words, the lack of choices implied by their shared oppression shapes Black women's behavior no less than Black men's. Davis goes on to explain:

> I hope you don't see this as an apologetic stance. I'm only trying to understand the forces that have led us, Black women, to where we are now. . . . A mother cannot help but cry out for the survival of her own flesh and blood. . . . Anxieties, frustrations engendered by the specter of a child dead of starvation focus our minds and bodies on the most immediate necessities of life. The "job" harangue, the "make yourself something" harangue. Exhortations grounded in fear, a fear brought into being and sustained by a system which could not subsist without the poor, the reserve army of unemployed, the scapegoat. (*Autobiography*, 372)

In the end, Davis agrees with Jackson that there is work to be done in Black women's learning to rechannel their energies into active resistance beyond the edict of survival. However, she cautions that this imperative is neither more nor less critical—in terms of the success of liberation struggle—than the need for Black men to resist capitulation to male privilege under patriarchy. At the same time that women must learn to take up the gun, then, men must be prepared to take up housework or the responsibilities of rearing children. Because a unified front requires the empowerment of daughters *and* sons, there is no room for counterrevolutionary gender expectations. According to Davis, Black women's entrance as soldiers in the revolution "presupposes that the Black male will have purged himself of the myth that his mother, his woman, must be subdued before *he* can wage war on the enemy. Liberation is a dialectical movement—the Black man cannot free himself as a Black man unless the Black woman can liberate herself from all this muck" (374). Gently calling attention to Jackson's failure to recognize the impact on the struggle of manifestations of sexism and/or misogyny, Davis applies to Black women's status vis-à-vis Black men the same language and logic Jackson himself apparently used in describing the relation between progressive Blacks and their reactionary counterparts. Davis writes: "Like you said, George, there are certain obvious criteria for measuring the extent to which counter-revolution is being nourished by those who call themselves our companions in struggle. Their attitude toward whites is one criterion. *Their attitude toward women, another*" (374; emphasis added). Davis insists that enemies of the struggle must be determined by how they come down not only on the issue of race, but also on the issue of gender. As an example, Davis criticizes LeRoi Jones (a.k.a. Amiri Baraka) and Ron Karenga, along with the other cultural nationalists, for their stance advocating "the total submission of the Black female as rectification for the 'century-long wrongs she has done the Black Male' " (374).

In essence, Davis's narrative revises Jackson's on the issue of gender by reestablishing a critical context for Black women's responses and experiences, something decidedly absent in Jackson's critique. As Jackson's understanding of his mother's particular reality (and, by implication, that of other Black women as well) deepens, and as he realizes genuine solidarity with Davis and other committed women activists, Davis's autobiography indicates that Jackson begins to recognize his earlier generalizations about Black women as essentialist and reductive. Significantly, the last letter in Jackson's collection suggests a noteworthy change in his attitude toward his mother, as he implores Joan [Hammer] to remove from the final manuscript "any references to Georgia being less than a perfect revolutionary's mama." Of course, Jackson's change in attitude toward his mother is probably also attributable to Georgia Jackson's own change in political consciousness, as well, and her subsequent advocacy on George's (and other political prisoners') behalf. (This information appears in Davis's autobiography as opposed to Jackson's.) In the letter addressed to Joan asking her to remove all unflattering references to his mother, Jackson indicates: "I want no possibility of anyone misunderstanding her as I did" (Jackson, *Soledad*, 247). The statement provides some perspective for evaluating the earlier letters. Jackson's narrative, when read alongside Davis's, reveals that Jackson's views about women, like his attitude toward his parents, evolve over the course of a dialogical process. Like the roll-call convention in activists' texts, Davis's inclusion in the autobiography of her letter to Jackson functions in the politics of mention by making available her half of their dialogue. Her autobiography, published in the wake of Jackson's *Soledad Brother*, helps to amend the historical record.

While reading the women's and men's narratives in tandem reveals compelling dialogues about gender and sexism (as evident in the dialogue between Davis and Jackson), reading recent narratives against earlier ones can also be illuminating. That is, not only do dialogues across gender revise each other, but newer texts revise the understanding of the era we have gleaned from earlier narratives. With the advantage of historical distance and the perspective that generally accompanies that, later writers like Elaine Brown and David Hilliard, for example, offer a very different picture of the Black Panther Party and the era that tends to deromanticize both in useful ways. Both explore some of the contradictions between Party ideology and practice. They also offer considerable insight into the psychological stress—the personal toll—associated with activist work under the constant threat of violent repression. For Hilliard and Brown, writing autobiography is furthermore an act of self-recovery. Because by their own admission both joined the Party in search of an identity rather than to actualize one in which they were already secure, their sense of self became inextricably bound to the direction and fate of the organization. Both remained with the Party, even through its most troubled years, in part because neither could imagine that there was any life for them outside of it. As Hilliard concedes: "The Party is home, where I am accepted; anyplace else is exile" (Hilliard and Cole, 309). In the aftermath of the Party's demise, each sought, to some degree, to recover a sense of self *apart* from their respective associations with the Party, which at one time completely subsumed their identity. Referring to the period between the time she left the Party and the time she actually began working on *A Taste*, Brown recalled in an interview that she was "either angry or crying all the time." Disillusioned with the direction of the Party in its final days, she lamented that her life seemed to be going back "to being valueless" (Graham, 32). Writing becomes her way of reinscribing meaning, of giving form and substance to a self. This move toward self-recovery, alone, distinguishes both texts from other revolutionary activists' narratives, which tend to move in the opposite direction (i.e., away from focus on the individual "I" toward identification with the collective "we").

Although Brown and Hilliard, like those writing before them, ultimately celebrate the integrity of the Movement, the Party's mission, and the righteousness of the organization's noblest ideals, neither appears overly concerned with upholding Party propaganda. Part of each one's political agenda, in fact, involves taking an honest inventory about where the Party sometimes went wrong. In *A Taste of Power* and *This Side of Glory*, multiple factors are shown to contribute to the Party's eventual decline. In *A Taste*, Brown points to increasing substance abuse by Newton and other members of his inner circle, internecine violence, and pervasive sexism as the primary factors precipitating the Party's demise. While Hilliard too notes these factors, *This Side of Glory* also explores external factors that were at work. He acknowledges, in particular, the impact on the organization of the FBI's counterintelligence program in the 1960s and 1970s, better known as COINTELPRO. Although the scope of COINTELPRO's activities targeting Black activists would have been publicly accessible information (i.e., through the Freedom of Information Act) by the time Brown began writing *A Taste*, Brown's decision to narrate past events through past consciousness likely accounts for the relative absence of information about COINTELPRO in her text. In place of retrospective analysis, she chooses merely to describe the program's effects, presenting them as they were experienced by herself and fellow Party members at the time. *This Side of Glory*, by contrast, repeatedly refers to police/FBI infiltration of the Party and the effects this had on Party morale and on the declining stability of the organization. Throughout the autobiography, Hilliard incorporates actual quotes from the COINTELPRO files that help to contextualize the unfolding of critical events in the Party's history. Moving alternately between past and present consciousness, *This Side of Glory* takes into account both how

Party members experienced COINTELPRO at the time (e.g., the paranoia and internal dissension its directives created) *and* what has been
learned in the years since.

In general, the documentary style of Hilliard's narrative enables him
to do things with his text that Brown and others before him could not.
In repeatedly turning the narrative over to other individuals (some of
whom are quite critical of his actions in the past), Hilliard creates an
autobiography in which his "I" is only one of several voices involved
in telling the story. Occasionally, there is tension between individuals'
differing recollections of the same event. This tension, which is fore-
grounded by the way conflicting recollections are deliberately juxtaposed
in the text, is purposely left unresolved. In this way, the story belongs
less to the individual than to the community; ownership is shared by all
who take part in the story's telling. Other voices fill in where the limitations of Hilliard's own memory (or of his willingness to share sensitive
information) become apparent. This allows his text to appear honest at
points where Brown's and others', for a variety of reasons (including
self-incrimination), must occasionally shut down. With multiple voices
telling the story, Hilliard is able to revisit a number of rather troubling
episodes in the Party's history in a way that moves his narrative substantially (though not entirely) beyond the propaganda recapitulated in
other activists' texts.

While Brown's narrative deromanticizes the Party's leadership by illustrating the corrupting nature of power, Hilliard endeavors to demystify some of the so-called "colossal events" that became an integral part
of Party lore and propaganda. Perhaps chief among these was the April
6, 1968, shootout between the Panthers and police that resulted in the
death of Li'l Bobby Hutton. In *This Side of Glory* Hilliard implies that
the shooting was less a case of police harassment (as alleged by the
Party and its supporters) than a direct response to Panther *provocation*
engineered by Eldridge Cleaver. According to Hilliard, Cleaver and
other Panthers involved in the incident (including Hilliard himself) had
originally gone cruising with the intention of ambushing a police car,
but their plan went awry (Hilliard and Cole, 187). They were stopped
by the police, and a shootout ensued in which Cleaver, Hilliard, Hutton,
and the other Panthers were quickly outgunned. Forced to flee into the
surrounding neighborhood, Hilliard found temporary shelter inside the

home of a sympathetic resident, while Hutton and Cleaver sought refuge inside a cellar. The latter, however, were quickly discovered by the police and forced to surrender at gunpoint. Although Cleaver survived the episode with bullet wounds to the leg and buttock received earlier in the shootout, Hutton was killed instantly while attempting to surrender (193). The frequency of *unprovoked* police violence against Panther members notwithstanding, Hilliard's narrative is the first autobiography to date to imply that the Party was at least partly culpable for the particular circumstances leading to Hutton's violent death.

Apart from the recasting of circumstances leading up to Bobby Hutton's death, Hilliard's autobiography also rewrites the highly controversial story of Newton's October 28, 1967, arrest for the shooting death of police officer John Frey Jr., in Oakland, California. The story of Newton's encounter with Officer Frey is one of those instances in which Hilliard turns the narrative over to another speaker. The story, as it is told in *This Side of Glory* by Gene McKinney, turns out to be at odds with an earlier version recounted by Newton himself in *Revolutionary Suicide*. Both Newton's and McKinney's accounts agree that Newton was driving the night he and McKinney were stopped by police, apparently without cause. Such routine police harassment was a recurring experience for most Black radicals during the time. Both men's accounts agree that more than one cop was involved and that Newton was shot in an ensuing scuffle between him and the police. Beyond this, the two versions offer significantly different details. The disparity could be attributable to any number of issues, from the revisionism of memory (presumably McKinney's recollections in *This Side of Glory* were recorded many years after the incident) to the fact that the statute of limitations (as Newton himself was fond of saying) never runs out on murder.

In Newton's version of the incident in *Revolutionary Suicide*, a second patrol car joined the first while he and McKinney waited in their car for the first officer to return Newton's registration. After conferring with each other, the officers ordered both Newton and McKinney out of the car. While McKinney was escorted by the second officer, Newton writes, the first officer (Frey) directed him toward the back of the second patrol car. During this time, he claims he was unable to see what was happening with McKinney and the second officer. As Newton and Frey approached the back of the squad car, Newton maintains that Frey struck him in the face, knocking him to the ground. Even as he went down, Newton insists that he was at the time still clutching the law book he had in hand when he was first ordered out of the car. As he attempted to rise, Newton recalls that the officer raised his revolver and fired, wounding Newton in the stomach. He claims subsequently to have heard a rapid volley of shots; disoriented by his own wounds, however, he writes that he could not determine their origin (Newton and Blake, 174–76). In Newton's version of the story, careful attention is devoted to each move he and Frey allegedly made. He is careful to note, for instance, where his own hands were at all times, his position vis-à-vis the officer's, the approximate distance he fell when struck by Frey, and even the precise position in which he landed as a result of the blow.

By comparison, Gene McKinney's version in *This Side of Glory* reads much more vaguely. It is unclear, for instance, whether the two cops arrived together or in separate cars. McKinney maintains, contrary to Newton, that he was still *inside* the car at the time the first shot was fired. Dramatically, he recalls:

> All of a sudden I hear this shot—BOOM! Oh man! Huey's out there! I jump out of the car. I don't worry about the weed or stuff. Huey's out there! I run back towards the police car, going by my instincts, seeing about Huey. Huey and one cop are entangled; the other cop is shooting. I grab Huey and he's hit. I think, "Hey! I got to get Huey out of here!" I start running across the street and I see a buddy of mine coming in his car and I flag him down and get Huey into the car and, boom! we shoot over to your [Hilliard's] house. (Hilliard and Cole, 131)

What is particularly interesting about the contrast between McKinney's version of the incident in *This Side of Glory* and Newton's in *Revolutionary Suicide* is that Newton's version implicitly sets up the possibility that McKinney could have shot Frey (he also leaves room for the other officer to have been the inadvertent killer), while McKinney's version implicitly denies this possibility. After all, by McKinney's account, *he* was still inside the car. Later in *Revolutionary Suicide*, Newton points to the lack of material evidence to implicate either himself or McKinney (187–88).

Incidentally, Newton's version of the attempted arrest does not mention the marijuana. McKinney's acknowledgment at the outset of telling the story that they "had a little weed in the car" must, of course, be placed in the context of 1970s countercultural norms: though still illegal, possession of marijuana then carried much less stigma than it has acquired in the 1980s and 1990s. This notwithstanding, drug use of any sort within the Party was supposedly strictly forbidden on the grounds that it impaired the clear thinking necessary to carry out revolutionary political work. Although Newton admits that marijuana allegedly found in the car driven by him and McKinney was entered into evidence against him when he was tried for Frey's murder, he is adamant in calling the drug charges against him bogus. Newton attempts to defend his innocence in the narrative by arguing that the drugs were planted by police. He further argues that, as head of the Party, he would never have been foolish enough to take such risks knowing not only the frequency with which Panthers were routinely stopped by police, but also that drug abuse was strictly forbidden inside the Party (Newton and Blake, 206). In light of Brown's revelations in A Taste, however, Newton's posturing can only be interpreted as disingenuous by contemporary readers asked to believe his story. If McKinney's recollections in This Side of Glory are, in fact, reliable, Newton's rhetorical question, "why would I take the risk?" (206) begs an answer. McKinney's casual admission of the marijuana becomes striking when contrasted with Newton's emphatic denial of the charges. That both Hilliard's and Elaine Brown's narratives attest to rampant substance abuse within the Party's ruling elite certainly casts serious aspersions on Newton's credibility in this instance. According to Brown, in the later years of the Party, Newton's erratic mood swings and behavior were often directly attributable to drug and alcohol abuse. Inspired by the twelve-step program that has become part of his own recovery from drug and alcohol addiction in the years since his affiliation with the Party, Hilliard commits himself in his autobiography to moving beyond the rhetorical dodge or the tendency to reframe situations so as to avoid personal accountability. Of course, the success of his endeavor can only be measured by the extent to which future (i.e., yet to be written) accounts of the period emerge to take issue with Hilliard's own recollections. That This Side of Glory retells the (legendary) stories of Bobby Hutton's murder and Newton's arrest provides a compelling illustration of the manner in which later narratives tend to complicate our readings of earlier texts.

Just as Brown's autobiography reveals information not found in the narratives by either Davis or Shakur, David Hilliard's narrative includes substantial information about the Party and its activities not found even in Brown's text. Dialogues that revise the story of the Movement appear across gender (as in the case of Davis and Jackson's correspondence) as well as across time. The point is that each writer reflecting on his or her own experiences tends to add something new and different to the telling of the Story, which ultimately works to enlarge our appreciation of the Movement, as well as of the activists involved. While the repetition of key events is critical to forging a counterhegemonic history, it is conceivable that the contradictions and contestations that also emerge could be read as undermining that history. However, I wish to argue the contrary: that such moments, rather than undermining this history, point to its complexity. Perhaps because I am not a historian, the contradictions that become apparent in reading Black Power activists' narratives intertextually are much more exciting than dismaying to me. After all, so long as individuals are vying for how they as well as the Story (or stories) of the Movement will be remembered, this history remains alive. The resonance created by reading the men's and women's, older and more recent, narratives in tandem makes apparent that the "long story of the people" (Silko, 6) and the Truth of the Movement are best captured when many people remember together.

Epilogue

The autobiographies by women activists of the Black Power Movement have much to offer readers as we approach the dawn of a new millennium. While progressive change has certainly altered the American social landscape since the turbulent 1960s and early 1970s, there is much work yet to be done toward the eradication of social injustice and inequality. Without constant vigilance and willingness to struggle against myriad forms of domination (including racism, xenophobia, sexism, and homophobia), the gains that many fought so hard for stand to be lost. In stressing the importance of critical literacy Davis, Brown, and Shakur call attention to the kinds of tools—oppositional knowledge and rhetoric—necessary to challenge structures of domination. As resistance literature, their narratives invite readers to interrogate hegemonic ways of knowing and understanding. Writing autobiography is a way for them to document their experiences, to give voice to the voiceless, to amend the historical record, and to expose repressive tactics of the state. Readers of their texts are encouraged to move beyond a complacency with the status quo in order to imagine alternative possibilities for what this world *might* be. If the value of their texts were to stop here, one might simply liken their merit to good, thought-provoking fiction, which after all has the potential to do much the same work. However, beyond challenging hegemonic values and assumptions, activists' narratives also advocate and model transformative action. Their texts insist upon the value and importance of linking theory with practice. The imperative and the challenge is to do something meaningful with the knowledge one gains. In this way, Davis's, Shakur's, and Brown's writing autobiography can be seen as an important extension of their political work.

What all three women share about the nature of their experiences in activist struggle should make clear that there can be no credible history of the Black Power Movement without the inclusion of women's voices. While it would be presumptuous to assume that their particular stories are representative of all or even most women who were on the front lines of the Movement, their narratives collectively suggest a range of experiences that are generally not accounted for in the narratives by their male counterparts. Their texts, for example, point to significant differences between the sexes in terms of how each negotiated gender-role expectations, parenthood, interpersonal relationships, and interaction with the dominant culture. Although reading the men's and women's narratives together reveals considerable overlap between their respective experiences, the kinds of obstacles and consequences each confronts leading up to and during her involvement in revolutionary struggle are sometimes very different. Davis's, Shakur's, and Brown's theorizing of their early/formative years speaks to some of these differences and also begins to illuminate the process(es) by which Black women become radical subjects in the context of race *and* gender oppression. In affirming the value of collective struggle for social justice while also exposing the ideologies and practices that undermined Black liberation struggle in the 1960s and early 1970s, the women's narratives can inspire as well as guide younger activists today in theorizing their own work.

Bibliography

Abu-Jamal, Mumia. "Live From Death Row." *The Progressive.* May 1995: 18+.

Andrews, William. "Toward a Poetics of Afro-American Autobiography." In *Afro-American Literary Study in the 1990s,* ed. Houston Baker Jr. and Patricia Redmond. Chicago: University of Chicago Press, 1989.

"Angela Davis Implicated in San Rafael Shootout." *Los Angeles Sentinel,* 31 August 1970: 1+.

Aptheker, Bettina. *The Morning Breaks: The Trial of Angela Davis.* New York: International Publishers, 1975.

Baireuther, Charles. "Maximum Security Probe Eyes Racism, Shootings." *Los Angeles Sentinel,* 20 August 1970: A3.

Baker, Houston A., Jr. *Workings of the Spirit: The Poetics of Afro-American Women's Writing.* Chicago: University of Chicago Press, 1991.

Bambara, Toni Cade, ed. *The Black Woman: An Anthology.* New York: Signet, 1970.

Baraka, Amiri, and the Afro-American Commission of the Revolutionary Communist League. *The Afro-American National Question.* 1979. Newark: Unity & Struggle Publications, 1992.

Barrios de Chungara, Domitila, and Victoria Viezzer. *Let Me Speak!* Trans. Victoria Ortiz. New York: Monthly Review, 1978.

Barsamian, David. "Right-Wing Take-Over of Public Broadcasting." *Z Magazine,* April 1995: 6–8.

Benjamin, Playthell. "The '60s Radicals: Where Are They Now?" *Emerge,* April 1991: 20–27.

Berkeley in the Sixties. Dir. Mark Kitchell. California Newsreel, 1990.

Bin Wahad, Dhoruba, Mumia Abu-Jamal, and Assata Shakur. *Still Black. Still Strong: Survivors of the U.S. War Against Black Revolutionaries.* Ed. Jim Fletcher, Tanaquil Jones, and Sylvère Lotringer. New York: Semiotext(e), 1993.

Blauner, Bob. "The Shadow of the Panther." Rev. of *The Shadow of the Panther: Huey Newton and the Price of Black Power in America,* by Hugh Pearson. *New York Times Book Review,* 10 July 1994: 1+.

Bond, Jean Carey, and Patricia Peery. "Is the Black Male Castrated?" In *The*

Black Woman: An Anthology, ed. Toni Cade Bambara, 113–18. New York: Signet, 1970.

Braxton, Joanne M. *Black Women Writing Autobiography: A Tradition Within a Tradition*. Philadelphia: Temple University Press, 1989.

Bray, Rosemary L. "A Black Panther's Long Journey." *New York Times Magazine*, 31 January 1993: 21–23 +.

"Brothers Arraigned in UCLA Slayings." *Los Angeles Times*, 24 January 1969: 1 +.

Brown, Elaine. *A Taste of Power: A Black Woman's Story*. New York: Pantheon Books, 1992.

———. "Attack Racism, Not Black Men." *New York Times*, 5 May 1993: Op-Ed.

——— et al. "Women and the Civil Rights Movement." *Talk of the Nation*, National Public Radio (NPR), 26 August 1993.

Chancer, Lynn. *Sadomasochism in Everyday Life: The Dynamics of Power and Powerlessness*. New Brunswick, N.J.: Rutgers University Press, 1992.

Christian, Barbara. "The Race for Theory." In *Making Face, Making Soul: Creative and Critical Perspectives by Feminists of Color*, ed. Gloria Anzaldúa, 335–45. San Francisco: Aunt Lute Books, 1990.

Churchill, Ward, and Jim Vander Wall. *Agents of Repression: The FBI's Secret Wars Against the Black Panther Party and the American Indian Movement*. Boston: South End Press, 1988.

———. *Cages of Steel: The Politics of Imprisonment in the United States*. Washington, D.C.: Maisonneuve Press, 1992.

Cleaver, Eldridge. *Soul On Ice*. New York: McGraw-Hill Book Co., 1968.

Cleaver, Kathleen Neal. "Sister Act: Symbol and Substance in Black Women's Leadership." *Transition: An International Review* 60 (1993): 84–100.

Cleaver, Kathleen, and Angela Davis. "Rekindling the Flame" [A dialogue moderated by Diane Weathers and Tara Roberts]. *Essence*, May 1996: 160.

Coleman, Kate. "A Death in Berkeley." *Heterodoxy* March/April 1995: 1 +.

Coleman, Kate, with Paul Avery. "The Party's Over." *New Times*, 10 July 1978: 23–47.

Dao, James. "Fugitive in Cuba Still Wounds Trenton." *New York Times*, 1 May 1998: B1 +.

Davidson, Joe. "Caged Cargo." *Emerge*, October 1997: 36–46.

Davies, Carole Boyce. *Black Women, Writing and Identity: Migrations of the Subject*. New York: Routledge, 1994.

Davis, Angela. *Angela Davis: An Autobiography*. 1974. New York: International Publishers, 1988.

———. *Women, Race, and Class*. New York: Vintage Books, 1983.

———. "Radical Perspectives on the Empowerment of Afro-American Women: Lessons for the 1980s." *Harvard Educational Review* 58, no. 3 (August 1988): 348–53.

———. "Black Nationalism: The Sixties and the Nineties." In *Black Popular Culture*, ed. Gina Dent, 317–24. A Project by Michelle Wallace. Seattle: Bay Press, 1992.

———. "The Making of a Revolutionary." Rev. of *A Taste of Power: A Black Woman's Story*, by Elaine Brown. *Women's Review of Books* 10, no. 9 (June 1993): 1+.

——— et al. *If They Come in the Morning: Voices of Resistance*. New York: New American Library, 1971.

Dillard, Annie. "To Fashion a Text." In *Inventing the Truth: The Art and Craft of Memoir*, ed. William Zinsser, 53–76. Boston: Houghton Mifflin Co., 1987.

Dougherty, Ed. "Witness Tells of Slaying—and Newton Laughing." *San Francisco Chronicle*, 26 October 1977: 2.

Erikson, Erik, and Huey P. Newton. *In Search of Common Ground: Conversations with Erik Erikson and Huey P. Newton*. New York: W. W. Norton & Company, 1973.

Eyes On the Prize: America at the Racial Crossroads, 1965–1985. Dir. Louis Massiah and Terry Kay Rockefeller. Videocassette. Blackside, 1988.

Fanon, Frantz. *Black Skin, White Masks*. New York: Grove Press, 1967.

———. *The Wretched of the Earth*. New York: Grove Press, 1968.

Foner, Philip S., ed. *The Black Panthers Speak*. New York: Da Capo Press, 1995.

Former Black Panthers Discuss Legacy of Movement. Transcript. Prod. Robert Malesky. *Weekend Edition/Sunday*, NPR, 18 July 1993. 5–10.

Foucault, Michel. *Discipline & Punish*. Trans. Alan Sheridan. New York: Vintage, 1979.

———. *Power/Knowledge: Selected Interviews & Other Writings, 1972–1977*. Ed. Colin Gordon. New York: Pantheon Books, 1980.

Franklin, H. Bruce. *Prison Literature in America: The Victim as Criminal and Artist*. New York: Oxford University Press, 1989.

Freeman, Mark. *Rewriting the Self: History, Memory, Narrative*. New York: Routledge, 1993.

Freire, Paulo. *The Politics of Education: Culture, Power, and Liberation*. Trans. Donaldo Macedo. Granby, Mass.: Bergin & Garvey, 1985.

———. *Pedagogy of the Oppressed*. Trans. Myra Bergman Ramos. New York: Continuum, 1989.

———, and Antonio Faundez. *Learning to Question: A Pedagogy of Liberation*. New York: Continuum, 1989.

Gates, Henry Louis Jr., ed. *The Classic Slave Narratives*. New York: NAL Penguin, 1987.

Genette, Gérard. *Narrative Discourse: An Essay in Method*. Trans. Jane E. Lewin. Ithaca, N.Y.: Cornell University Press, 1980.

Giroux, Henry A. *Teachers as Intellectuals: Toward a Critical Pedagogy of Learning*. Granby, Mass.: Bergin & Garvey, 1988.

———. "Literacy, Critical Pedagogy, and Empowerment." In *Schooling for De-*

mocracy: *Critical Pedagogy in the Modern Age*, 142–72. London: Routledge, 1989.

———. *Disturbing Pleasures: Learning Popular Culture*. New York: Routledge, 1994.

Graham, Reneé. "She Still Believes in Panthers." *The Boston Globe*, 22 February 1993: 30+.

"Guns Are Gone, but Former Black Panthers Still Idealistic." *Los Angeles Sentinel*, 14 April 1994: 14A. Ethnic Newswatch.

Gusdorf, Georges. "Conditions and Limits of Autobiography." In *Autobiography: Essays Theoretical and Critical*, ed. James Olney, 28–48. Princeton, N.J.: Princeton University Press, 1980.

Haley, Alex, and Malcolm X. *The Autobiography of Malcolm X*. New York: Ballantine Books, 1965.

Hall, Stuart Elwyn. "Panther Books Cause Group More Controversy." *Metro Reporter*, 23 May 1993: 1. Ethnic Newswatch.

Harding, Vincent. *There is a River: The Black Struggle for Freedom in America*. New York: Vintage Books, 1981.

Harlow, Barbara. *Resistance Literature*. New York: Methuen, 1987.

———. *Barred: Women, Writing, and Political Detention*. Hanover, N.H.: Wesleyan University Press, 1992.

Hatfield, Larry. "Marin Shootout Aftermath, A Key Question: Who Shot First?" *San Francisco Examiner* (Final Ed.), 9 August 1970: 1+.

Hilliard, David, and Lewis Cole. *This Side of Glory: The Autobiography of David Hilliard and the Story of the Black Panther Party*. Boston: Little, Brown and Co., 1993.

Hochschild, Adam. "His Life as a Panther." Rev. of *This Side of Glory*, by David Hilliard. *New York Times Book Review*, 31 January 1993: 7.

hooks, bell. *Ain't I a Woman*. Boston: South End Press, 1981.

———. "The Politics of Radical Black Subjectivity." *Z Magazine*, April 1989: 52–55.

———. *Talking Back: Thinking Feminist, Thinking Black*. Boston: South End Press, 1989.

———. "Black Women Intellectuals." In bell hooks and Cornel West, *Breaking Bread: Insurgent Black Intellectual Life*, 147–65. Boston: South End Press, 1991.

———. *Black Looks: Race and Representation*. Boston: South End Press, 1992.

———. *Teaching to Transgress: Education as the Practice of Freedom*. New York: Routledge, 1994.

Horowitz, David. "Black Murder, Inc." *Heterodoxy*, March 1993.

Jackson, George. *Blood in My Eye*. 1962. Baltimore: Black Classic Press, 1990.

———. *Soledad Brother*. 1970. New York: Bantam, 1972.

Jacobs, Harriet. *Incidents in the Life of a Slave Girl*. Ed. Jean Fagan Yellin. Cambridge: Harvard University Press, 1987.

James, Joy. "Teaching Theory, Talking Community." In *Spirit, Space, & Survival: African American Women in (White) Academe*, ed. Joy James and Ruth Farmer. New York: Routledge, 1993.

Johnson, Roy. *The Nat Turner Slave Insurrection* (Together with Thomas R. Gray's *The Confession, Trial and Execution of Nat Turner* as a Supplement). Murfreesboro, N.C.: Johnson Publishing Co., 1966.

Jones, Jack. "Second Brother Held in Slayings at UCLA." *Los Angeles Times*, 22 January 1969: 3 +.

Jones, Jacqueline. *Labor of Love, Labor of Sorrow: Black Women, Work, and the Family, From Slavery to the Present*. New York: Vintage, 1985.

Kaiser, Charles. *1968 in America: Music, Politics, Chaos, Counter-culture, and the Shaping of a Generation*. New York: Weidenfeld & Nicholson, 1988.

Karenga, M. Ron. "A Response to Muhammad Ahmad." *The Black Scholar* 9–10 (July-August 1978): 55–57.

Kihss, Peter. "Composites of 4 Issued by Police in Prison Break." *New York Times*, 5 November 1979.

Krupat, Arnold. *Voice in the Margin: Native American Literature and the Canon*. Berkeley: University of California Press, 1989.

Lejeune, Philippe. *On Autobiography*. Ed. Paul J. Eakin. Trans. Katherine Leary. Minneapolis: University of Minnesota Press, 1989.

Liberatore, Paul. *The Road to Hell: The True Story of George Jackson, Stephen Bingham, and the San Quentin Massacre*. New York: The Atlantic Monthly Press, 1996.

Lockwood, Lee. *Conversation With Eldridge Cleaver: Algiers*. New York: Dell Publishing Co., 1970.

Lorde, Audre. *Sister Outsider*. Freedom: The Crossing Press, 1984.

Lutz, Catherine. "The Gender of Theory." Unpublished manuscipt, SUNY-Binghamton, 1990.

Mandela, Winnie. *Part of My Soul Went With Him*. Ed. Anne Benjamin. Adapted Mary Benson. New York: W. W. Norton & Co., 1984.

Marable, Manning. *How Capitalism Underdeveloped Black America: Problems in Race, Political Economy and Society*. Boston: South End Press, 1983.

———. "Blueprint For Black Studies and Multiculturalism." *The Black Scholar* 22, no. 3 (1992): 30–35.

McCall, Nathan. *Makes Me Wanna Holler: A Young Black Man in America*. New York: Random House, 1994.

McCartney, John T. *Black Power Ideologies: An Essay in African-American Political Thought*. Philadelphia: Temple University Press, 1992.

Memmi, Albert. *The Colonizer and the Colonized*. Boston: Beacon Press, 1965.

Menchú, Rigoberta. *I, Rigoberta Menchú, an Indian Woman in Guatemala*. London: Verso Books, 1984.

Mills, Kay. *This Little Light of Mine: The Life of Fannie Lou Hamer*. New York: Dutton—Penguin, 1993.

Moraga, Cherríe. *Loving in the War Years*. Boston: South End Press, 1983.

Morgan, Janice, and Colette T. Hall. *Gender and Genre in Literature: Redefining Autobiography in Twentieth-Century Women's Fiction*. New York: Garland Publishing Co., 1991.

Morris, Aldon. *The Origins of the Civil Rights Movement: Black Communities Organizing for Change*. New York: The Free Press, 1984.

Morrison, Toni. "The Site of Memory." In *Inventing the Truth: The Art and Craft of Memoir*, ed. William Zinsser. Boston: Houghton-Mifflin Co., 1987.

"Murder Trial Maneuvering Delays Proceedings 2 Weeks." *Los Angeles Sentinel*, 10 July 1969: A1+.

Muwakkil, Salim. "Political Prisoner." *In These Times*, 10 July 1995: 18–19.

Nelson, Jill. "The Outsider's Inside Story." Rev. of *A Taste of Power*, by Elaine Brown. *Washington Post*, 1 February 1993: B2.

Newton, Huey P. *To Die for the People: The Writings of Huey P. Newton*. 1972. New York: Writers and Readers Publishing, Inc., 1995.

———. *War Against the Panthers: A Study of Repression in America*. New York: Harlem River Press, 1996.

Newton, Huey P., and Herman J. Blake. *Revolutionary Suicide*. 1973. New York: Writers and Readers Publishing, Inc., 1995.

Oppenheimer, Martin. *The Urban Guerilla*. Chicago: Quadrangle Books, 1969.

O'Reilly, Kenneth. *Racial Matters: The FBI's Secret File on Black America, 1960–1972*. New York: Macmillan—The Free Press, 1989.

Pearson, Hugh. *The Shadow of the Panther: Huey Newton and the Price of Black Power in America*. New York: Addison-Wesley, 1994.

Petry, Ann. *The Street*. Boston: Beacon Press, 1946.

A Place of Rage. Dir. Pratibha Parmar. With Angela Davis, June Jordan, and Alice Walker. Women Make Movies, 1991. 52 min.

Popp, Robert. "Kidnap and Escape Try Drama." *San Francisco Chronicle*, 8 August 1970: 1+.

Pugh, Catherine. "Elaine Brown: A Taste of Power." *Washington Afro-American*, 6 February 1993: B6. Ethnic Newswatch.

Reich, Wilhelm. *The Mass Psychology of Fascism*. Trans. Vincent R. Carfagno. New York: Farrar, Straus & Giroux, 1970.

Seale, Bobby. *A Lonely Rage: The Autobiography of Bobby Seale*. New York: Times Books, 1978.

———. *Seize the Time*. 1968. Baltimore: Black Classic Press, 1997.

See, Carolyn. "An Insider's Look at Black Panther Party." Rev. of *A Taste of Power*, by Elaine Brown. *Los Angeles Times*, 4 January 1993: E3.

Shakur, Assata. *Assata: An Autobiography*. Westport, Conn.: Lawrence Hill & Co., 1987.

———. Interview. "Like It Is." By Gil Noble. New York: WABC-TV, 1988.

Shakur, Sanyika. *Monster: The Autobiography of an L.A. Gang Member*. New York: Penguin, 1993.

Shor, Ira, and Paulo Freire. *A Pedagogy for Liberation: Dialogues on Transforming Education*. Granby, Mass.: Bergin & Garvey, 1987.

Silko, Leslie Marmon. *Storyteller*. New York: Arcade—Little, Brown & Company, 1981.

Sinclair, Abiola. "A Conversation with Elaine Brown: Author of *A Touch [sic] of Power*." *New York Amsterdam News*, 30 January 1993: 24. Ethnic Newswatch.

———. "*A Taste of Power*, A New Book About the Black Panther Party." *New York Amsterdam News*, 23 January 1993: 22. Ethnic Newswatch.

Smith, Sidonie. *Where I'm Bound: Patterns of Slavery and Freedom in Black American Autobiography*. Westport, Conn.: Greenwood Press, 1974.

———. *A Poetics of Women's Autobiography: Marginality and the Fictions of Self-Representation*. Bloomington: Indiana University Press, 1987.

Smith, Sidonie, and Julia Watson, eds. *De/Colonizing the Subject: The Politics of Gender in Women's Autobiography*. Minneapolis: University of Minnesota Press, 1992.

Stepto, Robert B. *From Behind the Veil: A Study of Afro-American Narrative*. Chicago: University of Illinois Press, 1979.

Stone, Albert. *Autobiographical Occasions and Original Acts: Versions of American Identity From Henry Adams to Nate Shaw*. Philadelphia: University of Pennsylvania Press, 1982.

Tyehimba, Cheo. "Panther Mania." *Essence*, February 1995: 108 + .

Van Deburg, William L. *New Day in Babylon: The Black Power Movement and American Culture, 1965–1975*. Chicago: University of Chicago Press, 1992.

Waite, Elmont. "Warden Says Judge Had No Chance." *San Francisco Examiner*, 10 August 1970: 1 + .

Walker, Alice. "They Ran On Empty." Rev. of *This Side of Glory*, by David Hilliard. *New York Times*, 5 May 1993: Op-Ed.

Wallace, Michelle. "Her Life at the Top." Rev. of *A Taste of Power*, by Elaine Brown. *New York Times Book Review*, 31 January 1993: 7.

White, Hayden. "Interpretation in History." In *Tropics of Discourse*. Baltimore: Johns Hopkins University Press, 1978.

Williams, Evelyn. *Inadmissible Evidence: The Story of the African-American Trial Lawyer Who Defended the Black Liberation Army*. New York: Lawrence Hill Books, 1993.

Woodson, Carter G. *The Mis-education of the Negro*. 1933. Hampton, Va.: U.B. & U.S. Communication Systems, 1992.

Young, Iris Marion. *Justice and the Politics of Difference*. Princeton, N.J.: Princeton University Press, 1990.

Index

4797